UNIVERSITY KEELE

STAFFORDSHIRE

LIBRARY

Please return by the latest date shown

-2. NOV. 1992		
25. JUN. 199		
~~CANCELLED~~ OC 2003		
04. JAN 2004		

D1486525

0 682 969 4

A Japanese View of Detente

A Japanese View of Detente

Hisahiko Okazaki

Published for the Atlantic
Council of the United States

Lexington Books
D.C. Heath and Company
Lexington, Massachusetts
Toronto   London

Library of Congress Cataloging in Publication Data

Okazaki, Hisahiko, 1930-
   A Japanese view of detente.

   An updated and abridged version of the work published in Japanese in
1971 under title: Kinchō kanwa gaikō.
   1. World politics—1945- I. Title.
D843.05313   327.52   73.20328
ISBN 0-669-92569-1

Copyright © 1974 by D.C. Heath and Company.

All rights reserved. No part of this publication may be reproduced or
transmitted in any form or by any means, electronic or mechanical,
including photocopy, recording, or any information storage or retrieval
system, without permission in writing from the publisher.

Published simultaneously in Canada.

Printed in the United States of America.

International Standard Book Number: 0-669-92569-1

Library of Congress Catalog Card Number: 73-20328

Contents

Foreword

Discussions of security questions in the post-World War II era have been either bilateral or regional in scope. In the economic sphere, multilateral interdependence has progressed at such a rapid pace that world institutions are struggling to keep up. But in security matters regional approaches still prevail. Nevertheless, we live in an era in which the politics of detente are taking on broader dimensions and such events as the SALT talks I and II, the conference on European security, the negotiations on mutual force reductions in Europe, the post-Vietnam conference on Indo-China and the many bilateral efforts can all be seen as pieces in the broader mosaic of global detente among the major powers. While there are important specific differences between European and Asian security perspectives, it is highly desirable that considerations of security, strategy, and detente be examined in a framework which includes Japan, Europe, and the United States.

This book provides a fresh and new perspective on this complex subject. The candid, thought-provoking views are especially timely and reinforce the global rather than the parochial approach. In keeping with this preference, the book is being sponsored by the Atlantic Council of the United States.

We are most grateful to Mr. Okazaki for his excellent analysis, his straightforward approach, and his delightfully personal style. The substantive views expressed are, of course, his and do not necessarily reflect the individual or collective thinking of the Council. *A Japanese View of Detente* is a remarkable book and we are pleased to present it for public consideration and debate.

Washington, D.C.

Henry H. Fowler
*Chairman, Atlantic Council of the
United States*

Preface

This is a skeptical book. It is skeptical in the sense that it presupposes human nature will not change its character in the coming decades, nor will the international community in any fundamental way. More specifically it bases its analysis on two likely prospects: probably during this century the world will continue to lack an effective supranational body and the authoritarian states will maintain their one-party dictatorial systems.

Practitioners of diplomacy and national security affairs like myself are trained to be cautious, and to be prepared for any contingency, including various kinds of pessimistic future prognoses. It is true that even planners of diplomacy and national security are often tempted to dwell on hopes or ideals in their analysis and in formulating policy, but they know by experience that if things turn out differently—most of the time they do—this analysis and policy would serve no purpose.

In my diplomatic career, my experience in detailed analysis of international affairs and policy planning is rather concentrated in the period between 1966 and 1970, when I was then in charge of the Analysis Division of the Japanese Ministry of Foreign Affairs and the policy planning staff. Even the experience of this short period provided ample grounds for being wary of uncritical optimism about the future.

At present, the word on many lips is "detente." Some people today actually believe that the Soviet invasion of Czechoslovakia could never be repeated, given the prevailing mood of detente, apparently forgetting that this was precisely what more than 90 percent of the experts in Communist affairs also believed until August 20, 1968. At that time, optimism was based on the conviction that the cold war had ended, that the prevailing mood of detente would prevent the Soviet leaders from repeating the harsh measures of the earlier Hungarian incident, and also that an invasion would further weaken the international Communist movement. In fact the mood of detente may have been even more prevalent in 1968 than in 1973.

There were quite plausible reasons, apparently cogent reasons to expect peaceful solutions to problems, yet things turned out very differently. Even now, as a diplomat, I feel very reluctant to prophesy or suggest policy based on the hypothesis that the Hungarian or the Czechoslovakian cases were the last of their kind.

Today, moreover, one hears even more optimism expressed about China. It is widely believed that the cultural revolution was a special, unique phenomenon, and that Chinese foreign policy will be more flexible and moderate in the future. This may or may not be true. I remember the same arguments were heard after the Korean War and after the Great Leap. It is worth remembering that almost none of the Chinese experts expected the cultural revolution in late 1965, and that most of them refused to believe what was happening even when the early signs of that revolution appeared.

I would not have the temerity to predict that either the cultural revolution or the Great Leap were the last events of their kind. I am reminded of the fact that, in the past, moderate periods in China as well as radical periods rarely lasted more than five years.

Today, many observers of international affairs say that Sino-Western detente will last as long as the Sino-Soviet conflict continues. Although this is an argument which carries considerable weight, caution is still in order. When we remember how few people predicted the Sino-Soviet rift in the 1950s, we cannot rule out the possibility that the situation might change radically once more, despite the near-unanimous prediction at present that this rift will continue for the foreseeable future and although Sino-Soviet rapprochement may seem no more than an Orwellian fantasy at present.

In this analysis, everything revolves around the problem of how to deal with Communist states. The unpredictability of the future stressed above is a special fact-of-life about Communist states, where a one-party dictatorial system and the strict control of opinion make it very hard for outsiders to follow the policy-making process and to predict policy shifts. Some people now deny the very concept of a special Communist modus operandi, and prefer to explain the foreign affairs of these states in terms of traditional power politics or even idealism. In my opinion this is inaccurate.

In post-World War II diplomacy we have learned never to lose sight of two basic elements underlying world politics: power politics and ideological confrontation. Power politics has always been an inherent element in diplomacy since the time nations and states came into existence. In fact, the wisdom in the history books, dealing with the ancient Greek states or ancient Chinese states, still remains true in many international phenomena. The reason why this obvious factor of power politics had to be borne in mind in the postwar years was the newly intensified ideological nature of East-West confrontation. In addition, idealism, symbolized by the establishment of the United Nations, dazzled us and tended to make us forget the importance of age-old truths.

It happens, however, from time to time in human history, that an element other than power politics plays a significant role in international politics. For example, it is not possible to explain international events during the Crusades without mention of the religious element, unless one is prepared to be labeled as a power-political monomaniac. Likewise, there is little doubt that future historians will characterize the period dating from 1945 to a certain future date by the peculiar phenomenon of ideological conflicts between Communist and non-Communist worlds. In spite of talk about "the end of the cold war," very few experts will yet admit that ideological conflict has ceased to be one of the fundamental elements characterizing contemporary world politics. In fact, when we discuss detente or peaceful coexistence, we mean detente or peaceful coexistence between Communist and non-Communist states, thus presupposing the basic difference between the two systems.

In this book, I have tried to illustrate the history of hope alternating with terror, the expectation shattered by frustration, and new hope and endeavor born out of despair, during the last twenty-five years of East-West relations. If the reader beings with the awareness that detente is such a complex question that it should not be dealt with lightly, then much of my purpose is already accomplished.

This book is a translation of one published primarily for Japanese readers by the Japan Institute of International Affairs in 1971. It has been updated and abridged since that time to make it as pertinent as possible without altering its substance. It represents my private views, I should point out, and is in no way the official position of the Japanese government.

Finally, I owe deep gratitude to the people who rendered invaluable assistance to the completion of my book. In addition to the people in Japan already acknowledged in my book in Japanese, I wish to express my thanks to members of the Atlantic Council who undertook to publish this book under its aegis and, in particular, to Dr. James F. Sattler, for his professional help. I am also grateful to Professor Richard Walker for his scholarly advice and Ms. Jan Monson for her assistance.

1

The Paradox of Detente

What Is Tension?
What Is the Relaxation of Tension?

In this chapter we stress the complexity of the concepts of tension and the relaxation of tension. Generally speaking tension is regarded as bad and its relaxation as good. Taking the example of human relations in regard to tension, however, hundreds of questions can be raised. Is a complete relaxation of tension possible between two individuals? Might it not be better to have some tension or at least a certain courteous reserve between them? Can you trust a person with a relaxed attitude more than a tense person? Might not a calculated, relaxed attitude be more dangerous than frankness? In order to attain a durable friendship, which of the two attitudes is more constructive, friendly words and gestures, or blunt frankness, which might be interpreted as tension?

Detente is perhaps the vaguest, the most ill-defined term in modern diplomacy. On the other hand, we may safely state that present East-West tension has undoubtedly been reduced from what it was in the early days of the cold war. If we do not recognize this historical fact and stress only the indefinability of detente, then we will never go beyond a futile game of words. Let us examine some actual cases in the postwar period.

Case of the Cuban Crisis

What kinds of forces have worked to achieve the present state of detente? While we can count many significant elements since the death of Stalin, I believe that most experts would agree to include the Cuban crisis as one of the most important events.

The Cuban crisis resulted in the relaxation of tensions in two senses. First, in a short-term and local sense it relaxed the tension in the Caribbean. The Soviet intention of installing missile bases in Cuba was abandoned, while Cuba gained some assurance that the United States would not seize the island by force. Thus elements which might have produced military confrontation in that area were eliminated, and at least temporary relaxation of tension in the Caribbean was achieved. It may be a temporary solution, but it has already lasted more than a decade.

Second, the crisis led to a longer term and far more important result. The

Cuban crisis confirmed by deed the official Soviet decision not to risk full-scale nuclear warfare against the United States, and thus opened a new horizon of genuine dialogue between the United States and the USSR on the question of nuclear balance. The following decade was one of dialogue and agreement on the question of the maintenance of mutual nuclear deterrence and nuclear disarmament. This began with the partial test ban treaty of 1963, was followed by the nonproliferation treaty, and culminated in the SALT negotiations. Moreover, in deciding to avoid a nuclear war, one has to avoid a situation which is likely to lead to a nuclear war. Thus there was also a development of mutual understanding between the two superpowers on the problems of local conflicts which were not directly connected with the nuclear balance, but were likely to disturb international equilibrium. In the style of Confucius' *Spring and Autumn*, a book of history characterized by its brevity of description and its austere and bold abstraction of cause and consequence, we may be allowed to say that U.S.-Soviet peaceful coexistence of the 1960s began with the Cuban crisis.

One lesson of the Cuban crisis is that at some stage of bilateral relations it is useful for both sides to indicate to each other a clear picture of what may or may not be conceded. A firm attitude sometimes brings about better communications and eventually genuine peaceful coexistence and detente. In this case, the firm attitude meant the "quarantine measure" by President Kennedy. It implied that the United States was determined to eliminate the missiles in Cuba by all possible means.

Obviously we cannot call President Kennedy's measure a detente policy or a policy for relaxing the prevailing tension. In fact, tension reached the highest point ever in the postwar period for several days after the declaration of the measure. What would have happened if the United States had taken measures which did not formally contradict the policy of relaxation of tension and had avoided the threat or use of force? Certainly the short-term heightening of the tension would have been avoided. Cuba would have received the missiles and remained under the constant threat of American invasion or preemptive attack. The Caribbean would have remained as a high tension area and possible area of U.S.-Soviet confrontation right up to the present. Then the peaceful coexistence we have now would not have been achieved, or would have required another crisis, confrontation, and perhaps a still higher level of tension in Cuba or in some other area of the world.

A much quoted and perhaps stereotyped example is the appeasement policy of Chamberlain on the German annexation of Sudetenland. The appeasement policy was based upon the overwhelming support of the British public opinion at that time. But it proved to be only the postponement of an eventual confrontation. And now it is generally thought that the firm attitude shown at the time of the invasion of Poland should have been shown when Sudetenland was occupied. Some people remind us of the antiwar declaration of the Oxford Union in 1933, which said that the British would not take up arms "for king and country." They say that Hitler quoted this declaration whenever the chiefs-of-staff of the German army warned against a new adventure. This is regarded as a case where an antiwar movement did not help relax world tension, but actually encouraged a war.

The Case of the Berlin Wall

In order to stress the complexity of the problem, let us consider a still more controversial example.

In early 1970, the prime ministers of West and East Germany met for the first time after the partition. Since then, East Germany has been gradually recognized as an international entity by Western nations, but it is undeniable that the main reasons for this development were that East Germany became the most prosperous and stable economic society among East European countries in the middle of the 1960s, and that the Western nations, including West Germany began to recognize this fact. Why did East Germany become such a prosperous and stable country? The Berlin Wall played a significant role in this.

At the beginning of the 1960s East Germany appeared to be on the verge of disintegration as a nation and as a society because the most productive part of its population kept fleeing to West Germany through Berlin. The Communists suddenly built the wall in August 1961, creating tension which, at its height, was nearly comparable to the Cuban crisis.

Although it is undeniable that this wall-building brought about stability in East German society, as well as economic success and possibly detente on the East-West dividing line, one hesitates to call it a detente policy. Consider the time element. While the short period of tension in the Cuban crisis was instrumental in bringing about a long lasting period of U.S.-Soviet peaceful coexistence, the Berlin Wall created mistrust and disgust for a decade and resulted only in a possible beginning of detente. Moreover, it may be argued that the latent discontent of the East German people, suppressed by the physical limitation of the wall, may someday engender a new crisis and tension.

Nevertheless, the wall opened a long process of recognition of or resignation to the status quo by Western nations, above all by the West German people. It is hard to tell now whether the Soviets would have risked a war on the question of the wall, or more fundamentally, on the question of the separate existence of East Germany. But if so, the Soviets forced the recognition of the status quo by drawing a line between what they could concede and what they could not.

Case of Detente Diplomacy

A more fundamental paradox will be found in "detente diplomacy" itself, which will be examined below. It is seen in the two alternative views of Western policy towards East Germany in the long process of the recognition of the status quo of a divided Germany. The prosperity of East Germany even now owes a great deal to the fact that it shares in the prosperity of the EEC through commercial exchanges with West Germany. One view suggests that by broadening economic contacts with East Germany and raising its standard of living East Germany would be encouraged to accelerate further its economic growth and would inevitably adopt a freer economic system and eventually even a freer social system. According to a second way of thinking, the East German economy narrowly escaped exposing the bankruptcy of its socialist economy, like other East European nations in the 1960s, only by its trade with West Germany. So far, the second assessment is identical to the first. However, the second view suggests that broadening trade between the two Germanys would only help the conservative doctrinarians and harm the position of liberal reformers in the East German regime. Furthermore, if the Western nations continue the existing policy of economic intercourse, East Germany could not only maintain its policy but also use the material resources thus gained for activities harmful to West Germany, for example, winning the favor of the third world countries competing with West Germany. (It is interesting to note that similar arguments were made in regard to Japanese cooperation in Siberian development.)

The Czechoslovakian incident of 1968 can be analyzed with regard to these two alternative views. Correlation between the Western detente policy and the Czechoslovakian invasion, however, poses a very difficult problem. As will be explained in Chapter 3, it is wise to refrain from drawing too direct a cause and effect relation. Nevertheless, we can generally assume that the stability of the European situation under peaceful coexistence and detente since the last third of the 1950s prompted the Czechoslovakian people to seek a higher standard of living, a more effective economic and social system, and a higher degree of intellectual freedom. The short springtime of Prague could not possibly have been realized without this historical background. The "Prague Spring," however, invited Soviet invasion and threw Europe into a period of chill under the Brezhnev doctrine. We might outline one pattern of contemporary historical process in which the relaxation of tension, as it develops and goes beyond what Soviets cannot tolerate, introduces a period of high tension by inviting Soviet intervention. Of course, an optimist will say that the world is still proceeding towards the relaxation of tension, following a zigzag course in the long run. This may be true, but human life is too short for the toleration of subjugation and humiliation, simply because they are seen as part of a temporary reactionary period.

Summary

The above examples may have overstressed the complexity of the problem of relaxing tensions in international affairs. I felt it necessary, however, to stress what seems to be an almost oversimplified approach in view of the current trend of thinking. Diplomacy should always be flexible. As soon as it is bound by a slogan it departs from the real national interest. Relaxation of tension is a good thing, but one should not use it as the only yardstick for assessing a measure taken by a government.

For example, there is a usual presumption that an East-West dialogue is a good thing and a break in communications is a bad thing. Likewise the opening of a talk is a good thing and its suspension is a bad thing. Thus opening or reopening the Paris talks on Vietnam, and Warsaw talks with China in the 60s, was welcomed as a step towards relaxation of tension, and its suspension always was deplored, being termed as an aggravation of tension. Where Western nations are shackled by this popular concept, the Communist side can easily draw both real advantages and propaganda advantages by simply suggesting opening or suspending a meeting. Sometimes they can even gain substantial concessions from the Western side in return for simply agreeing to enter into negotiations. In a democratic society, where relaxation of tension has popular support, a government can make domestic political gain out of it even if the government makes unilateral concessions outside. The value of negotiation should depend on its result. Dialogue without result may sometimes be useful, particularly when there has been no previous communication, but it is not worth unilateral concessions.

Relaxation of tension is a welcomed state, but careless or superficial use and application of the term "detente" to international politics may have adverse effects, such as, neglecting the fundamental security of a nation simply because there is a formal logical contradiction between the notion of security and that of detente; giving priority to the national interests of countries other than one's own by urging too much "peaceful gesture"; or giving importance to the immediate posture or words rather than to their long-term effects in maintaining peace and security.

The most expressive comments on the superficiality of the notion of relaxation of tension may be found in Chou En-lai's Report to the Tenth National Congress on August 31, 1973. Chou said: "Must China give away all the territory north of the Great Wall to the Soviet revisionists in order to show that we favour relaxation of world tension? . . ."

After all, diplomacy is diplomacy. Whether it is called detente diplomacy or peace diplomacy, it should be based on the correct assessment of the situation and, hopefully, deep insight into the future. Diplomacy is a matter of how to make the best choice in a given circumstance for promoting the national interest within the framework of world peace and prosperity. Detente diplomacy is only a facet of such overall diplomacy. It is necessary always to be aware of the complexity of diplomacy when assessing foreign policy.

Detente Policy as Tactics

There is another element which adds further complexity to the already difficult notion of detente. Detente policy is very often employed for almost exclusively tactical purposes. The simplest method is to put one's opponent off guard by assuring him of the peaceful intention of one's side. A classic example is that of the battle of Osaka in 1614-15. The Tokugawa shogunate was then trying to complete its national hegemony by seizing the Osaka castle, the last stronghold of the Toyotomi Clan. Having found it difficult to seize it by force, the Tokugawa side proposed a peace whereby both Tokugawa and Toyotomi would remain as friends on condition that the Toyotomi would let the Tokugawa bury the deep moat around the castle, which, according to Tokugawa, would serve no purpose under the friendly relation of the two powers. The Toyotomi side agreed, and was exterminated in a renewed battle several months later.

There are innumerable similar examples in the history of the world. The application of this tactic in the special circumstance of East-West confrontation in the postwar world is evident in much modern propaganda. A typical example I have called "the peace offensive."

Peace Offensive

The peace offensive of the Soviets was opened full scale around 1949. The propaganda was based on the theory that the United States was preparing an aggressive nuclear war against the socialist countries and organizing a war-mongering military alliance in West Europe. Conversely, the Soviet Union was heroically fighting for peace against this imperialist design. For its propaganda, Moscow mobilized all Communist front organizations and sympathizers, and also succeeded in gaining the support of many of the intelligentsia in the Western world. It had them hold international "peace meetings" in the main cities of the world, and had them adopt "peace appeals." A particular success was marked by the Stockholm Appeal adopted in March 1950 by the World Congress for the Defense of Peace (later called World Peace Council) established in April 1949. It was claimed that the Stockholm Appeal succeeded in collecting five hundred million signatures in the short period of eight months.

As a major effect of this peace offensive, many intellectuals in Western Europe and Japan came to believe that the Soviet Union was under the severe pressure of a military threat from the Western side and, above all, that the strengthening of Western Defense capabilities and alliances would provoke the USSR and be detrimental to the promotion of peace—in spite of the fact that the Soviet divisions on the eastern side of the iron curtain then outnumbered the Western divisions in Europe by almost ten to one, and that Communist parties in Paris and Rome advocated cooperation with the Red Army in case of eventual invasion in Western Europe. The documents show no Western design of preemptive nuclear warfare against Russia. The threat was obviously from the Eastern side, but propaganda partially succeeded in making some people believe the contrary.

As a matter of historical record, the formation of the NATO alliance brought about first the security of Western Europe, then economic and social stability, practical elimination of the fear of total warfare, peaceful coexistence and detente. But the deep influence of the peace offensive has lived in the minds of intellectuals in Western Europe and Japan for the long postwar period. Some people still insist that the act of concluding, revising, and maintaining the U.S.-Japan Security Treaty provokes Communist nations and produces an adverse effect on the relaxation of tension. Some further argue that Japanese participation in various Asian regional organizations will provoke Communist states and aggravate tension in the area. In these cases, particularly in the period between 1960-1970, the pattern of the peace offensive was repeated, in which a Communist state criticized Japan in its official media and some segments of the Japanese population joined in the criticism.

From the strategic point of view of a Communist state, stability and mutual cooperation of non-Communist states, including Japan, meant a comparative disadvantage for Communist influence in that region. So it was natural for the Communists to propagandize against them. Suppose Japan refrained from participating in these regional groups in order to avoid "aggravation of tension," what kind of concession would Japan have received from the Communist side? Very likely none. It is clear from the example of NATO that a better choice for Japan is to help these Asian nations attain their security and prosperity, and thus contribute to long-term stability, peace, and eventually detente of that area. For the sake of strengthening the people's liberation movement, a socially and economically unstable Asia would be more welcome than a stable one. In that case we should clearly recognize that there still exist conflicting interests between Japan and a Communist state. Here is a case where we should apply the principle of not giving priority to the national interest of another country rather than our own simply in order to achieve a short-term relaxation of tension.

Some Thoughts on Tactics

The peace offensive initiated by the Soviets in 1949 consisted of words only and was not accompanied by any substantial offer of concessions for peace. This fact was soon perceived by Western leaders and the peace offensive did not succeed in altering any substantial part of Western policy, even though it had a considerable effect on public opinion. Therefore, the peace offensive should be more accurately described as tactics than as an actual detente policy.

When trying to weaken the position of the opponent, there is a tactical question of whether a firm posture or a soft posture would better produce the desired result. The peace offensive itself can be described as a shift from the former firm posture. In the period when Europe was ravaged by war and the social situation was still unstable, the Russian hard line must have produced the effect of further shaking social stability by making people believe in the imminence of Communist revolution or Russian invasion and creating an apprehensive mood among the population. However, the coup d'etat in Czechoslovakia, and other developments in East European capitals, alarmed the West, the Marshall Plan was initiated, Western Communist parties started to decline as a result, and the peace offensive was begun, largely to allay fears about Soviet intentions.

Generally speaking, propaganda by posture works best when it is directed against an open society by a centrally controlled state. It should be always borne in mind that in propaganda warfare Western societies are at a disadvantage in dealing with Communist societies. Particularly when there is a division of opinion concerning the posture of the government, as there usually is in an open society, the Communist side can help deepen the division of opinion and thus weaken the bases of the government. For example, at the time of concluding the Japanese-Korean Treaty in the mid-1960s, some segments of the Japanese population argued that the establishment of the normal treaty relation with South Korea would provoke the suspicion of the Communist states about a possible Northeast Asian alliance and thus heighten tension in the Far East. The Communist states could support such segments of people by simply escalating their denunciation of the treaty, thus fulfilling the prophesy—and proving that their warning was right. This kind of tactic is hard for Western pluralistic societies to employ toward a Communist society where freedom of speech is restricted and division of opinion is hard to detect.

However, the problem of the choice between a hard posture and soft posture also exists in the strategy of Western diplomacy. In the absence of public opinion there is still a possibility of division of opinion within the leadership of a one-party system government. The simple and quite effective model is the dove-hawk relation. A soft posture on the Western side will encourage Communist doves and a firm posture will give warning to hawks within the Communist government. On the other hand a soft posture may encourage hawks and a firm posture may disillusion doves and weaken their position within the government. Prior to the halting of bombing North Vietnam by President Johnson, there was an argument that doves in the North Vietnam government had been advocating a negotiated settlement and that the American gesture of stopping the bombing would encourage the doves and bring North Vietnam to the conference table. Also, at the time of the Czechoslovakian invasion in 1968, there was an argument that a tougher American posture was needed for deterring Russian intervention. Although both of these arguments appeared to have proved right, it is difficult to tell whether the decision in the centralized regime was made in line with the process suggested by the above suppositions.

In such cases the object to which these postures are directed is not public opinion, but the leadership which possesses an extremely great ability to discern the real intention of Western governments. Therefore, Western postures need to be combined with certain realities. Unlike the peace offensive of Communist countries, which consists of words, the posture of the Western countries should accurately convey their real intentions to Communist countries. In other words, it is essential for the West to clearly define the conditions for detente and to reach a satisfactory compromise between interests of East and West. In that sense policy should not be called "posture" or "propaganda," but be thought of as well-conceived diplomacy itself.

Peaceful Coexistence, Detente, and
Propaganda

With the passing of time, Soviet policy has evolved from the peace offensive to peaceful coexistence, as the Western nations adopted detente diplomacy. Since both peaceful coexistence and detente diplomacy have far more complex significance than simple propaganda, and since they are the main theme of this book, they will be discussed in further detail in the following chapters. However, in East-West relations in the postwar period, all policy possesses a facet of propaganda, and we should never underestimate that facet.

In the vast theoretical structure of Khrushchevian peaceful coexistence there is an emphasis on the struggle to defend peace, which greatly resembles the earlier Stalinist peace offensive. This point will be elaborated below.

The detente diplomacy advanced by the Western nations possesses an element of an idealistic approach aimed at a lasting peace transcending the difference of East and West from the Western point of view, but it may be viewed by the Communist side as aiming for the short-term effect of loosening solidarity of Socialist nations and the long-term effect of transforming the Communist system itself, nothing more than the tactics and propaganda strategy of the capitalist camp. This point will be elaborated in Chapter 3.

2

Peaceful Coexistence

Method of Study

"Peaceful coexistence" is no longer a technical term, but one which is widely used. According to the common interpretation of the word, it means that the capitalist world and Communist world exist side-by-side on this earth and maintain peaceful relations between them. This is a fine definition and I do not think experts will object to it. Various problems arise, however, if we look into this definition more closely in connection with actual foreign policy.

From the Western side the main problem is the interpretation of Communist intention. Since the term "peaceful coexistence" was first used by the Communist side, the question always remains on what condition and how far the Communist side wants to be peaceful. The main problem on the Eastern side is how to accommodate the notion of peaceful coexistence to the framework of the theoretical structure of Marxism-Leninism. In fact, these two questions are actually the same, viewed from different angles.

The ultimate external policy objective of a Marxist-Leninist country is to achieve world revolution through class struggle; the possible use of violence cannot be excluded at some stage for achieving this objective. As will be seen later, no Marxist-Leninist can deny the above two principles although they often employ devious language to avoid direct quotation on these principles. This fact must mean that "coexistence" has to be temporary and "peaceful" relations should be conditional and have exceptions. Thus it requires a theoretical gimmick to accommodate the notion of peaceful coexistence with these principles.

If we apply Lenin's way of thinking directly, the purpose of peaceful coexistence is to take a breath and to gain time for strengthening the effort of building up socialism for a Socialist country which is completely surrounded by imperialism. This means that the Communist side observes peaceful coexistence while its strength is inferior to the capitalist world.

It is an objective fact that the total Communist military capability is still inferior to that of the Western world. In terms of theory, although Khrushchevian concepts of peaceful coexistence might have added "a substantially new content" to the Leninist way of thinking at one time, in recent years they have been withdrawn and Leninist quotations again predominate in current fundamental theoretical Communist documents. If we take it at its face value, the Communist side is building up its strength while gaining time under the policy of

11

peaceful coexistence and is waiting for the chance for the world revolution. Based on fundamental Leninist strategy, the Western world should have reason to expect large-scale war unless it can maintain decisive deterrent capability over the Soviets until such time as they abandon their Leninist approach.

On the other hand, the world situation has certainly changed since Lenin's time, while Communist states, for some understandable reasons, may have to keep explaining everything according to Leninist principles. Nuclear weapons, above all, did not exist in Lenin's time. This phase of East-West confrontation took a form which Lenin would have never dreamed of. Krushchevian peaceful coexistence can be construed as an antithesis of the Stalinist cold war. It is an objective fact that the East-West relationship now is different from that of the cold war period.

After all, the detente and peaceful coexistence which we are dealing with are nothing more than what the governments on both sides of the East-West confrontation professed and actually did in the period from the beginning of the 1950s to the present time. Since the term "peaceful coexistence" was first employed by the Communist side and theoretically elaborated by the Communist side, this chapter tries to explain the meaning of peaceful coexistence by analysing what the Communists said and did. Concerning the method of study there are two problems: (1) in the evolving definitions of peaceful coexistence, which period we should take as a base, and (2) to what degree the explanation given by the Communist side can be trusted as their real intention?

The Basic Period

As the basic period, this book takes the period of Khrushchev for Russia and the period of "Bandung diplomacy" for China, and tries to explain subsequent evolution up to now. In both periods peaceful coexistence was the most openly articulated theme in the foreign policy of the two countries. In the case of the USSR we have to avoid being buried in Communist literature by going into the Leninist and Stalinist periods. On the other hand it is hard to find in the Brezhnev period such a thing as a theoretical structure of peaceful coexistence. In the case of China, the period of Bandung diplomacy was also the only period in which the Chinese peace diplomacy as a whole was theoretically explained.

Real Intention of Communist Theory

To separate truth from propaganda in a Communist statement is a basic and frequently vexing problem as long as the Communist states maintain a one-party, dictatorial system.

Very few speeches were more discussed than the speech of Khrushchev at the

Twentieth Party Congress in 1956, which expounded the whole structure of the policy of peaceful coexistence. Most of its background is still a mystery. In that speech, Khrushchev stated that peaceful coexistence is not a tactic but a fundamental policy of Russian diplomacy. By saying that it is not sufficient that countries of different social systems simply should coexist as neighbors, but should go further in full strength to improve mutual relations and strengthen mutual confidence, he referred to the possibility of going beyond mere coexistence under mutual nuclear deterrence. He also referred in the same speech to the possibility of avoiding a war and to the possibility of parliamentarianism as one of the alternative ways to socialism in different countries. In comparison with the official Communist documents in the later period it contained remarkably progressive and reformist ideas. These ideas bore a distinct resemblance to those of such early revisionists as Bernstein and Bauer. Thus there was some justification for the Chinese' later charges that Khrushchev was a "revisionist."

It is natural, however, that the Western experts reacted with the utmost caution because the speech contained such a vastly different idea from that of Stalin. Of course we can never verify the real intention of Khrushchev. As many experts pointed out at that time, the main purpose may have been propaganda. In fact many parts were clearly designed for propaganda purposes. It is the habit of policy planners and practitioners of diplomacy to use the most cautious interpretation if there is any doubt about it. Many experts, however, who were very cautious at that time, now tend to admit that Khrushchev's ideas were somewhat more progressive than those of other Russian leaders, including his successors.

This is the tragedy of a closed society. In dealing with a country like the Soviet Union, where the process of decision-making is kept in extreme secrecy, one has to keep guessing the real intent and has to rely on the most careful assessment when the question is related to matters of security. Moreover, in facing a monolithic system it is always necessary to take into account the potential for sudden policy changes. Even if we had believed Khrushchev's intent to be sincere and had accepted his word, we still would have had to keep a margin of safety considering the capacity for sudden change in Soviet policy or leadership. In fact, Khrushchev fell and his words are no longer heard.

The cases of Russian individuals are more tragic. Some Russians, like diplomats or government or party officials, who have received an excellent political education, sometimes state their progressive opinions very freely. The objectives may be sometimes for exchange of information, sometimes for propaganda, or for gaining some political advantage by taking their counterpart off guard. On the other hand, Russia is a great nation which produced people like Tolstoy and Dostoyevski and still possesses enormous potential for producing great men. Some people do speak the truth, despite all the risks for their own and their family's safety and future. For the people who live in Western society it is extremely difficult to assess each individual who suddenly emerges from the closed society, and to evaluate how true his words are. Thus we may have a tragedy in which we treat an honest person with suspicion, counterposed against another tragedy in which we are taken advantage of by trusting a false friend. We remember that Khrushchev burst into anger in the United Nations and elsewhere. We still do not know whether it was a propaganda gesture condemning Western imperialism or genuine anger deploring the insensitivity of the Western side to his sincerity.

It is correct to say that we have to eliminate suspicion to secure a stable peace. However, it is wrong to say that, as a matter of policy, we have to throw out suspicion first. It is an historical fact that Soviets committed breaches of many nonagression pacts, and that the Chinese used force at the Sino-Indian border. It is false to assume that these actions could have been avoided by eliminating suspicion beforehand and by trusting the Communist states. The main thing is first to eliminate the condition which gives rise to suspicion. What detente policy is aiming at in the long term is exactly a situation where both sides can develop mutual trust.

Returning to the method of analysis in this book, the best way to verify true intentions is, of course, a careful case study to find out if words were really practiced in deeds. However, there are not always sufficient cases to test all words spoken in international politics. It is particularly useful to remind ourselves that nuclear deterrence is conditioned by a capability which is not supposed to be used, so any case study is by its nature impossible. In absence of cases to study, the documents of Sino-Soviet dispute are extremely useful. In the dispute the Soviet Union and China staked their prestige on their ability to epitomize Marxist-Leninist states. While they are obviously trying to keep a propaganda posture towards the outside world, they sometimes get emotional and quite often express their intentions with real candor. The best example is that of China, which stated in effect that peaceful coexistence cannot be more than tactical. In circumstances where neither case studies nor Sino-Soviet disputes can give clues, we have to make an assessment by an analysis of actual behavior in international politics.

Khrushchevian Theory

The foreign policy structure of the Soviet Union during Khrushchev's time was centered on peaceful coexistence. The easiest way to introduce this vast policy structure would be to explain it in accordance with the language of the Khrushchev speech at the Twentieth Party Congress in 1956. In this way, however authentic it may be, we would be lost in Communist phraseology and propaganda. Instead, to reach the heart of the question in each paragraph, let us use the Chinese classification or criticism, that is the idea of "Three peaces and two entireties." "Three peaces" means peaceful coexistence, peaceful competition, and peaceful transition. "Two entireties" means a nation of an entire people and a party of an entire people. For the Chinese these five points are, however, not intended to be a description of all Soviet foreign policy, but rather a list of Soviet "crimes" in the name of Marxism-Leninism. Be that as it may, by adding two aspects to which the Chinese are not opposed, "struggle for defending peace" and "struggle for people's liberation," the conceptual framework of Khrushchevian peaceful coexistence can be seen in its entirety. We could also add "the class struggle in the advanced countries," but this will be considered as another aspect of "peaceful transition" and is therefore omitted.

All of the other aspects are interrelated. Peaceful transition is the problem of achieving world revolution under peaceful coexistence. Peaceful competition is the question of the form of East-West rivalry under peaceful coexistence. The struggle for defending peace is the method—propagandistic method—of defending peaceful coexistence. The people's liberation movement poses the question whether oppressed people should observe peaceful coexistence. This book tries to explain all these problems item by item.

Peaceful Coexistence

The professed purpose of the Soviet Union's peaceful coexistence is very clear and very often repeated. According to Khrushchevian principles peaceful coexistence will increasingly receive wide international support. This, it is believed, is natural, because there is no other way under existing circumstances. One alternative is peaceful coexistence and the other is the most destructive war in history. There exists no third alternative. This attitude of choice between peaceful coexistence and a totally destructive war is repeatedly expressed in the Sino-Soviet dispute. The quotation below is the clearest example of this Russian attitude, although the Russian intention of playing up the Russian peaceful attitude in comparison with the Chinese is quite obvious.

Chinese comrades clearly underestimate the danger of thermonuclear warfare. They say that the most important thing is to destroy imperialism as soon as possible and it is a secondary question how and with how much sacrifice it will be achieved. Tell us, secondary for whom? For hundreds of millions to be killed by thermo-nuclear warfare? For the countries to be wiped out in the first few hours of the war? ... The atomic bombs do not discriminate between laborers and capitalists. They strike everywhere. For one monopolistic capitalist, millions of laborers will be killed. Laborers will question such revolutionary talk and ask "What kind of right do you have to solve our problems of survival and class struggle?" We want socialism, not with nuclear warfare, but through the class struggle.[a]

[a]Open Letter of the Central Committee to all Party organizations and all Party members, *Pravda*, July 13, 1963.

Do the case studies of the Cuban crisis, the partial test ban treaty negotiation, and the nonproliferation treaty negotiation assure us that the Soviets are telling the truth in this respect? We have to examine two problems to determine whether the above Soviet attitudes are really genuine.

First, peaceful coexistence is supposed to be based on the terrible destructiveness of nuclear weapons on the whole world, but it is also based on the fact that the United States still maintains an aggregate nuclear capability superior to that of the USSR. It is natural that the weaker party wishes to avoid a war. This is more a Leninist attitude than new policy under the new situation of the nuclear age. Moreover, the Soviets did not mention peaceful coexistence when they themselves did not possess sufficient nuclear capability, presumably because they did not opt to admit their decisive strategical inferiority. Therefore, Soviet peaceful coexistence is based on the circumstance in which they have already a second strike capability even though still inferior to the United States. Now the question is what the Soviets' attitude would be if they attained parity or superiority. This question is underscored by the recent announcement of Soviet MIRV tests.

Two answers are possible to this question. Some may expect that the USSR will try to expand its global influence towards the goal of world revolution, using its nuclear arsenal as the effective threat, even at the risk of a war. Others consider that even if nuclear capability increased nuclear weapons will remain "unusable" and thus deterrence can continue to stabilize peaceful coexistence. Under the conditions of U.S. nuclear suffieiency we trust that peaceful coexistence will be stable. However, we can expect a serious impact if the Soviet Union achieves a significant breakthrough, nuclear, conventional, or technological, and suddenly emerges as the number one superpower.

A second question is that of the contradiction between the principle of peaceful coexistence and other Marxist-Leninist principles. Most Chinese criticism of the USSR approach to peaceful coexistence deals with this question and therefore it is worthwhile to examine the Chinese attitude on peaceful coexistence.

The Chinese attitude toward nuclear weapons has shown a surprising consistency from the time of the first atomic bomb until the present U.S.-Chinese detente. In the opinion of the Chinese, the nuclear weapon is no more than one of several newly invented weapons which have appeared in human history from time to time. History is made not by a newly invented tool but by the will of the people.

In 1945 atomic bombs were dropped on Hiroshima and Nagasaki. Only a few days later, that is two days before the Japanese surrender, Mao Tse-tung, still in the caves of Yenan, observed:

Can we decide a war by an atomic bomb? No, we cannot. If we have only atomic bombs and no people's war, the atomic bombs mean nothing. Some of our comrades are committing a mistake in believing the atomic bombs to be a big thing. Why do they believe the atomic bombs to be a magical thing? It is because of the influence of bourgeois ideology. All the theories of the "weapon only" and the habit of looking at things from a simple military point of view derive from bourgeois ideology.[b]

Official Chinese literature elaborates on this point:

It is necessary to think how many people will die if war breaks out. The 2.7 billion population of the world may be diminished by one-third or even half. . . . In an extreme case, I would like to say that half of mankind will die, half will remain, but the whole world will be socialist and, within some years, the world will have 2.7 billion or more in population once more.

Some people believe that mankind will die out by a nuclear war. In practice this means that we have no other alternative than being subjugated by the nuclear threat policy of imperialists. Our comrade who struggles with us against this way of thinking, is the realization that the future of mankind is bright even if, in an extreme case, half of mankind should die in case imperialists start nuclear warfare.[c]

This way of thinking may have come from the confidence gained by its experience in the anti-Japanese war in which the Chinese Communists were not conquered by the modern Japanese army. One might even notice a trace of Oriental thinking in which they view the world continuously in transition—live things will perish sooner or later, new lives will be born and the truth will remain forever. From a purely strategic point of view, one might point out that the Chinese would not be able to afford any other attitude in their absolutely inferior status in nuclear strategy. It is also true that at one time Stalin said similar things. In this sense we have yet to see whether the Chinese attitude will change in the future.

Here is a typical example of Chinese theory on nuclear weapons at the peak of the Sino-Soviet dispute. The *People's Daily* dated December 31, 1962, refuting Togliatti and others on three counts, points out that:

There are three differences between us and people who criticize us.

1. The first question is whether the fundamental principle of Marxism-Leninism on the question of the peace and war has become outmoded by the advent of the nuclear weapon. Togliatti and others say, "the nature of a war has changed," or "the definition of just war should be reconsidered." . . . We continue to believe that there exist just wars and unjust wars under the principles of Marxism-Leninism. We are against the attitude of bourgeois pacifism.

2. The next question is whether we should take a pessimistic attitude on the future of mankind or take a revolutionary optimistic attitude. Togliatti and others consider . . . "It is senseless to discuss the future social system for the part of mankind who will survive the war." . . . We are opposed to this reasoning.

[b]Speech of Mao at the Party cardre meeting on August 13, 1945.

[c]As reported in the *People's Daily*, September 1, 1963.

3. Togliatti and others say, "it is natural to be frightened" by the nuclear threat and "A war should be avoided at any expense." . . . We believe that the American nuclear threat could fail and be frustrated by the concerted struggle of various forces who defend the peace. . . .

This quotation is so clear and self-explanatory that I do not think it necessary to elaborate. I simply wish to point out, from the strategic point of view, that only the first two points are relevant and the third point is more in the nature of propaganda.

The third point consists of calling up all peace-loving forces for the struggle against nuclear warfare. I do not think that the Chinese themselves believe in its effectiveness. The movement to stop nuclear war by antiwar and antinuclear forces was initiated by the Russians and is still continued by them on a greater scale than by China. From a strategic point of view, the theory of peaceful coexistence is based on the choice between peaceful coexistence and totally destructive war. It is a theory for the eventuality that the struggle for the defense of peace will be unsuccessful and the world will really be faced by the above alternatives.

Some people say that the Chinese theoretical position has shifted since the above quotation was made and that the Chinese are stressing the destructiveness of nuclear weapons more. Although it is very hard to find solid proof for this contention, it is not hard to find words indicating that the Chinese Communist party considers that the nuclear weapon has an unprecedented destructive power, and that a nuclear war would bring about unprecedented destruction to mankind. This reasoning was given, for example, in advocating a total nuclear test ban treaty. But in this case, as in most of the other cases, the thought is usually followed by the standard proviso that nuclear weapons cannot change the law of historical evolution of human society and cannot decide the final outcome of a war.

In 1972, during the General Assembly session of the UN, the Chinese Vice-Minister of Foreign Affairs said: "As everyone knows, war is the continuation of politics. The invention and development of nuclear weapons have not changed, nor can they change, this truth. . . . But now the Soviet government asserts that in a nuclear age there is no other way than peaceful co-existence among states. . . ."

Now let us turn to the general question of how to settle the contradiction between the principle of peaceful coexistence and other Marxist-Leninist principles. According to the language of Sino-Soviet dispute it is a question of whether peaceful coexistence is a strategy or a tactic. Strategy here means a long-term policy and is used in the sense of a fundamental policy. If peaceful coexistence is the fundamental policy of the international Communist movement, all other principles must be subordinated to the principle of peaceful coexistence.

The Chinese are opposed to the idea of taking peaceful coexistence as a fundamental policy. They say that unconditional coexistence means in practice continuous compromise with and continuous concession to imperialism. The result will be the reverse of peaceful coexistence. Therefore it is a mistake and is anti-Marxist and anti-Leninist. The Chinese insist that if peaceful coexistence were the fundamental policy, they would have to obey every imperialist demand under the threat of nuclear blackmail.

Then how should they deal with imperialism? According to them, by strategically despising the enemy and tactically respecting him. By despising the enemy strategically, they can avoid defeatism. This represents a belief that war (or revolution, since for Maoists they are the same) can be won by the side which has the support of the people. As long as they have the support of the people, they are afraid of nothing, because the final victory is always theirs. On the other hand, to avoid adventurism, or reckless action, they have to respect the enemy tactically.

The typical argument of the Chinese revolutionary is that, one must deal with individual cases most seriously and cautiously, and pay the utmost attention to the art of the revolutionary struggle. Without this consciousness, one will face failures and cannot lead the revolution to victory. And the Chinese say, in general, that the attitude held consistently by the Chinese Communist party is that the imperialists and all reactionaries are paper tigers. For them this is a completely Marxist-Leninist attitude. In the early 1960s the Chinese Communists were caricatured in Eastern Europe as well as in Asia as the people who insisted on calling the United States a paper tiger. But if we understand their theoretical terminology, we see that their revolutionary doctrine had a quite solid Maoist philosophy behind it. Perhaps the only mistake they committed was to have tried to force typical Maoist language unconditionally on people outside the Chinese world.

Soviet theory is, as we have repeatedly mentioned, the choice between total destruction and peaceful coexistence. Therefore, it has to be fundamental policy. However, from time to time the Soviets try to adjust this principle to the other revolutionary principles. Sometimes they say that there are three exceptions to this principle; these are ideology, class struggle, and the colonial liberation movement. They also maintain that these struggles should be based on the principle of peaceful coexistence in the present nuclear age. It is easy to point out the illogicality of the Soviet attitudes. However, as we examine actual cases which are likely to happen, we may be reasonably assured that peaceful coexistence can stand as the fundamental principle in theory and practice. The Soviets maintain that there will be no peaceful coexistence on the question of ideology. On this point both Soviets and Chinese are unanimous. In practice ideological confrontation takes the form of verbal disputes, inside and outside of an ideological bloc, and is not likely to bring about a nuclear war. The class struggle and people's liberation movement have the possibility of developing first into a civil war and then a local war, which might eventually endanger the peace of the world, but in past cases these struggles have been contained on a limited scale so that they would not create an overall East-West confrontation. Therefore, peaceful coexistence in its extremely limited sense of avoiding a nuclear war could well be the fundamental policy of Soviet foreign affairs in its practical application.

There is, however, one important point worth attention. Since the fall of Khrushchev it has become theoretically doubtful if peaceful coexistence is still fundamental in Russian foreign policy. A comparison of the 1962 and 1967 editions of *The Fundamentals of Scientific Communism*, a textbook for Soviet Communist party members, makes the difference clear. In the recent edition, peaceful coexistence is given a very low priority. The theory of the inevitability of war has been practically eliminated and the new stress is laid on the Leninist distinction between a just war and an unjust war.

The difference is also clear between the speech of Khrushchev in the Twentieth Party Congress in 1956 and that of Brezhnev in the Twenty-third Party Congress in 1966. Khrushchev stated that above all peaceful coexistence is not a tactical move but the fundamental principle of Soviet foreign policy, that socialism will win not by exporting revolution but by the superiority of its productive system. He added that it is not sufficient simply to coexist, but the world should proceed toward improvement of relations, mutual confidence, and cooperation. He further denied the fatalistic inevitability of a war and referred to different paths to socialism, including the possibility of using parliamentarism.

The Brezhnev speech, on the other hand, first stressed the struggle for consolidating the world system of socialism and strengthening its influence, above all the solidarity of the world Communist movement; second, it supported the people's liberation movement; third, it stated the measures to counter imperialist aggression; and finally it mentioned the struggle for the development of peaceful cooperation of various nations. Even in the last part it contained no explanation of peaceful coexistence. No wonder many Western experts on Russia have talked about so-called re-Stalinization in the past several years!

Thus, in spite of the current flowering of US-Soviet detente, theoretically speaking, we can assume that the policy of peaceful coexistence has lost its status as a fundamental policy of Soviet foreign policy. The practical meaning of this development is a very hard question to decipher. If we follow formal logic faithfully we could conclude that the Soviets will not avoid a nuclear war in order to maintain the "gains" of socialism in East Europe. This deduction follows from the Soviet's official position which gives higher priority to the solidarity of Communist forces than to the principle of peaceful coexistence. One might point out that this theory is proven by the Russian invasion of Czechoslovakia under the Brezhnev doctrine, the banner of the solidarity of the Socialist camp.

However, while it was Brezhnev who invaded Czechoslovakia, it was Khrushchev who invaded Hungary. Of course, in both cases they must have calculated that these invasions would not bring about nuclear wars. If we follow the logic of Khrushchev's speech in 1956 and that of Brezhnev in 1966, we might arrive at the conclusion that, in case there had been a real possibility of nuclear war, Brezhnev would still have risked war and Khrushchev would not have. The reality is not, of course, as simple as this. Looking back upon the actual circumstances, Khrushchev's action was more risky than Brezhnev's since the prospect of the impact of the invasion on East-West relations was less certain in the case of Hungary than of Czechoslovakia.

After having gone through all the theoretical aspects of peaceful coexistence we have come to the point where we have to ask ourselves once again, what is nuclear coexistence? We can assume that the Russian intention to avoid nuclear war is a genuine one and has been proved by various treaty negotiations from the partial test ban treaty to the present SALT, all through Khrushchevian and Brezhnevian times. But, it does not necessarily mean that the United States and the Soviet Union would never use nuclear weapons. If the possibility of their usage is eliminated, they are no longer a deterrent capability on which the total structure of peaceful coexistence rests.

How far could one side pursue its national interest or ideological interest without risking a nuclear war? One would never know. Neither the United States nor Soviet Russia would concede its vital interests. We may presume that each side would opt for a nuclear war rather than becoming a slave of the other. In this respect their attitude may be clearly different from that of some pacifist philosophers. Coming down to a more concrete example, what happens if Russian mechanized divisions start invading the whole of Western Europe? If it is expected that the Western side will defend itself only with tanks and airplanes, it means that there is no nuclear deterrence. According to the existing rules of the game it is supposed that the Western front in Europe is probably the place which may produce nuclear warfare. Even in that case everything depends on the circumstances. After the Cuban crisis President Kennedy is reported to have said to a friend that he was afraid Americans may believe from now on that the Russians would always withdraw before a show of force. This time they withdrew because the U.S. had a better case.

Then comes the question of peripheral conflicts. There are many peripheral conflicts around vital interests. Some of them may be considered almost as sensitive as the vital interests themselves. Moreover, a peripheral interest, which at first was thought to be dispensable, at any time could grow into a vital interest by escalation. It happens in the Japanese game of *go* that a slightly forced move at the very beginning of the game escalates itself into a situation which decides the entire game.

At this point we move beyond ideological considerations and become involved in game theory. Game theory is beyond the province of this book, but I will comment briefly on it here. Game theory in the more traditional sense involved the standard (non-ideological, non-nuclear) power relationships between great nations. The strategy between them is aptly described by Sun-tzu as, "War is the supreme matter of a state, the point of life and death, and the way to survival or perishing."

However, the fate of a nation or race, the choice of war or peace in the modern age, cannot be permitted to be decided by a theory or an ideology. The centuries old wisdom of mankind is the only appropriate guide. This also applies to the Chinese. In spite of their apparently reckless ideological stand, I do not believe that the final decision of peace or war will be dependent on an ideology.

Peaceful Competition

In his report to the Twentieth Party Congress, Khrushchev said:

When we say that the socialist system will win in the competition between the two systems—the capitalist and the socialist . . . our certainty of the victory of communism is based on the fact that the socialist mode of production possesses decisive advantages over the capitalist mode of production.

In a sense, this concept of peaceful competition truly formed the central position in Khrushchevian peaceful coexistence.

According to the Khrushchevian theory, the Russians will never give up the objective of world revolution but will try to achieve it within the framework of peaceful coexistence through class struggle in advanced countries and through the people's liberation movement in the underdeveloped world. However, I would like to draw attention to the theory which appeared at the time of Khrushchev: among the various kinds of revolutionary forces, the decisive victory will go to the most advanced force; the most advanced force is the world Socialist system, i.e. the international labor class and its product; the Socialist system is therefore the leading edge of the process of revolution. This theory was interpreted as meaning that the role of primary importance belongs to the existing Socialist system, above all the Soviet Union. Another interpretation is that the most important thing is to build up and strengthen the Socialist system and that the people's liberation movement should be subordinated, if necessary, to this supreme necessity.

How can the strengthening of the Soviet Union, not the people's liberation movement or the class struggles, play the central role in the world revolution? Here I quote the "Open letter of the central committee to all party organizations and all party members," published in *Pravda*, July 13, 1963.

The Soviet Union's persistent struggle for peace and international security, for general and complete disarmament, for the elimination of the vestiges of World War II, for negotiated settlement of all disputable international issues, has yielded fruit. The prestige of our country throughout the world stands higher than ever. Our international position is more solid than ever. We owe this to the steadily growing economic and military might of the Soviet Union, and of other socialist countries, to their peaceful foreign policy.

To insure peace means to contribute most effectively to the consolidation of the socialist system, and, consequently, to the growth of its influence on the entire course of the liberation struggle, on the world revolutionary process.

The letter further impresses on all workers of the world that Marxism-Leninism is a superior system to that of the capitalist world. To substantiate this proposal, the extraordinary Twenty-first Party Congress in 1959 presented a seven-year economic program and the new program in 1961 showed the Soviets passing the United States in industrial production by 1970 and raising the per capita productivity to double that of the United States standard, as well as surpassing the United States in all spheres of production by 1980. By 1970 all these plans had proved to be castles of sand. Contrary to the plan, the 1960s turned out to be the period when the Socialist economy faced various fundamental problems and needed radical reforms, while the free world experienced ten golden years headed by the remarkable progress of the Japanese economy.

The problem of the Socialist economy is a vast subject and this book will not discuss it. We might note here, however, that the optimism about the future of Socialist economy in the late 1950s, symbolized by the success of Sputnik, was the mainstay of the peaceful coexistence strategy of Khrushchev. If peaceful coexistence is not a short-term tactic and is almost a permanent arrangement, defeatism will result unless the Communist side is confident that it can win in peaceful competition. At the time when economic optimism moved from the East to the West, somewhere in the middle of the 1960s, it was natural that the focus of East-West relations shifted from the Soviet strategy of peaceful coexistence to the detente policy of the Western nations. Incidentally, in the Brezhnev period the notion of peaceful competition has been rarely mentioned in official Soviet documents.

Peaceful Transition

Peaceful transition is a problem which touches the roots of the international Communist movement. It is natural that various countries with different historical, geographical, political, social, and economic conditions take different roads to achieve socialism. The Russian revolution itself is an unorthodox case, considering that Marxism expected a revolution in the most advanced capitalist country. Lenin himself was well aware of this problem. According to Lenin who was quoted by Khrushchev in his speech at the Twentieth Party Congress:

All nations will arrive at socialism—this is inevitable, but all will do so in not exactly the same way; each will contribute something of its own to some form of democracy, to some variety of the dictatorship of the proletariat, to the varying rate of socialist transformations in the different aspects of social life.

Here we have two major problems; a problem with the countries which have not yet achieved the Socialist revolution and a problem of building up socialism in the nations which had already achieved a Socialist revolution.

Concerning the possibility of peaceful transition in the countries which have not yet achieved the Socialist revolution, Khrushchev stated, at the Twentieth Party Congress:

At the present time, the present situation offers the working class in a number of capitalist countries a real opportunity to unite the overwhelming majority of the people under its leadership and to secure the transfer of the basic means of production into the hands of the people. . . . In these circumstances, the working class . . . is in a position to defeat the reactionary forces opposed to the popular interest, to capture a stable majority in parliament, and transform the latter from an organ of bourgeois democracy into a genuine instrument of the people's will.

Of course, he adds an inevitable reservation as a Marxist-Leninist:

Leninism teaches us that the ruling classes will not surrender their power voluntarily.

As we have seen, even Khrushchev did not rule out the possibility of the use of force. In summary, revolution is hard to achieve without violence, as Lenin taught us, but this does not deny the possibility of peaceful transition in some cases. At present most Communist parties in advanced nations are taking the same line.

We have to be careful of this stance, though, because even this has a substantial propaganda aspect. The Communist parties in advanced countries say that it depends on the attitude of the capitalist side whether they will be forced to use violence after gaining majority support of a nation. If we look into the history of the Socialist revolution, however, the historical facts are exactly contrary to what they say. In the Russian revolution the Bolsheviki were a clear minority in the preceding elections, but seized power with use of violence. The coup d'etat in Czechoslovakia in 1948 was a case in which a government was socialized based on a free election, by the use of military force. In the case of the Czechoslovakian and Hungarian invasions we can see no majority support among the population for inviting Soviet troops. From these precedents, we have to assume that as long as Communists call themselves Marxist-Leninists they will act in the same way in similar circumstances as they did during the Russian revolution.

In the Sino-Soviet dispute China denies even this limited possibility of peaceful transition. Sometimes China supports the Soviet theory with the embarrassingly frank expression that in view of the current situation of the international Communist movement, it is useful tactically to bring in the hope for a peaceful transition, but it is inappropriate to stress the possibility too much. In simpler words, China says that in the circumstance where revolution is not immediately feasible, it may be profitable to talk about peaceful transition for the tactical purpose of putting the enemy off guard and expanding popular support for the Communist party. It is rather an exposure of the truth than support for the Russian position, and one can easily imagine the embarrassment on the Russian side. China gives as the reason for opposition to peaceful transition, the feeling that "empty words of peaceful transition will paralyze the revolutionary will of the people."

The Chinese are also opposed to peaceful transition even when they recognize the principle of peaceful coexistence. They say that peaceful coexistence is a state-to-state relation and does not apply to cases in which the people destroy the ruling class or the people stand up against foreign imperialist forces in colonial or semi-colonial states.

The Chinese are very firm on this matter. Mao consistently thinks that "The central task and the highest form of revolution is to seize power by armed force, to solve problems by war." This may be the frank thinking of a revolutionary who achieved revolution only through battle. It may be a realistic way of thinking, discarding all unreliable hope and illusions.

In following what each side said in the Sino-Soviet disputes it may look as if the Soviets are much more moderate than the Chinese. However, even during the Khrushchevian period, in the process of polemics against China, the USSR was made to recognize that there are both peaceful and nonpeaceful methods of revolution, and that both sides recognize that the chance of peaceful transition is not very great. In addition, peaceful transition is not referred to frequently in Brezhnev's time. Therefore, we can safely assume that at the present stage both countries think of the problem of transition to socialism very much along the lines of the Leninist idea of revolution by violence.

Now let us turn to the problem of the countries who have already achieved the Socialist revolution. According to Marxist theory, after achieving a Socialist revolution the next step is progress toward Communism, but at present all the states which have achieved Socialist revolution are defined as at the stage of socialism-building. If so, it follows that these countries can still take different roads in their endeavor to build socialism. In fact, Khrushchev's main aim was considered to be on this point, for enabling rapprochement with Yugoslavia. Khrushchev referred to Yugoslavia in the speech given at the Twentieth Party Congress:

In the Federal Republic of Yugoslavia, where state power belongs to the working people and society is founded on the public ownership of the means of production, specific concrete forms of economic management and organization of the state apparatus are arising in the process of socialist construction.

This theory of the different roads for building socialism opened the way to Soviet-Yugoslavian rapprochement but, in less than one year, it became a cumbersome burden on the Soviet leadership as a result of the Poznan riots and the Hungarian incident. The USSR invaded Hungary and its relations with Yugoslavia were again chilled.

This theory of the different roads to socialism remained in conflict with the principle of the solidarity of the Socialist camp. During the Prague Spring in 1968 there were polemics between the two party ideologues, Cisař of Czechoslovakia and Konstantinov of the USSR.[d] At that time Czechoslovakians were talking about the renaissance of Marxism and indulging themselves in free thinking, going back to the original ideals of Karl Marx, and referring to Leninism as a Russian version of Marxism. Naturally the Soviets were infuriated. In the polemics which followed, Cisař defended himself by quoting the theory of the different roads to socialism. The Soviet side could not effectively refute this. The polemics ended without result—and the armed intervention occurred in August.

History might repeat itself. So long as the Western side maintains hope for a true detente between East and West Europe, it should also be prepared for the probability that a conflict between Socialist solidarity and the theory of different roads to socialism will take place, creating tension once again in the future.

Two Entireties

Before moving to other aspects of peaceful coexistence, it may be in order to look at the question of the two entireties, that is a nation of an entire people and a party of an entire people, which I mentioned earlier, because this problem is closely connected with the theory of peaceful transition. Moreover, since it is a problem of social evolution within the Soviet Union rather than in other countries, it is more related to detente policy discussed in the next chapter than to peaceful coexistence.

In Khrushchev's report to the Twenty-second CPSU Congress on October 18, 1961, he said:

With the victory of socialism and the country's entering a period of building communism, the working class of the Soviet Union has at its own initiative and stemming from the tasks of building communism, transformed the state of its

[d]The exchange between academician F. Konstantinov and KSČ CC Secretary Čestmir Cisař was published, respectively, in *Pravda*, June 14, 1968 and *Rudé Pravo*, June 22, 1968.

dictatorship into the all-people's state/state of the whole people/. . . . For the first time a state has been formed in our country which is not the dictatorship of a certain class, but the weapon of all society, of all the people.

The Soviet purpose in proposing this theme is considered to be partly for Party reform and partly for propaganda. The fact that both Russia and China are under a party-type dictatorship has not changed at all, but the word "dictatorship," an authentic Marxist-Leninist term, gives a bad impression to the outside world. Making the assumption that exploitation by class difference no longer exists in Soviet Russia the Soviets have decided simply to state that the proletariat dictatorship has completed its historical role. It may follow from the Russian definition that Russia no longer needs a severe Socialist educational program within her borders. According to the Chinese, however, a sustained and intensive class struggle is necessary even within a Socialist state, because there still remain the leftovers of capitalism and new bourgeois elements keep coming up. The Soviets are making fun of the Chinese theory saying, "What kind of political scientist can create social classes of juvenile delinquents or extortionists?" I do not think it necessary to go into these polemics in depth, because after all, what both of them are doing is essentially the same, that is, conducting intensive Socialist education in schools and severe control of freedom of expression.

Incidentally, the term "proletarian dictatorship" disappeared from the new Party program which the Japanese Communist party adopted at its Eleventh Party Congress in July 1970. This may be interpreted as an effort to improve the image of the Party, but it brings about more theoretical problems than in the Soviet case. The Soviet Party program strictly limits the scope of its application by saying "in the case of the Soviet Union, from the standpoint of domestic development. . . ." Thus the USSR makes an exception of domestic affairs in the Soviet Union, but other countries should continue to apply the principle of Marxism-Leninism. This is logical. The JCP has not achieved a revolution and on that point differs from the Russian Party. The JCP might take parliamentarism or the united front tactic in dealing with other political parties at present and, after completing the process of revolution, might reach a "state of an entire people" like the Soviet Union. However, between these two stages they could not possibly achieve a Marxist-Leninist revolution without going through a period of proletarian dictatorship, a euphemistic name for Communist party dictatorship. In the case of the Party program of the JCP, it does not say that the historical role of proletarian dictatorship has ended. Therefore, it may be proper to interpret the new program as simply omitting any referrence to such dictatorship, primarily to improve the Party in the eyes of the Japanese population. In fact the recent Communist gains in Japanese elections are said to be, in large measure, a result of the Party's improved image.

Struggle to Defend Peace

At the Twenty-second Party Congress Khrushchev stated that peaceful coexistence can be maintained only by the antiwar peace movement's struggle for defending peace. He said:

Thus, the peaceful coexistence of states with different social systems can be maintained and secured only by the selfless struggle of all people against the imperialists' aggressive strivings.

This "peace appeal," or "appeal to all people of the world," adopted by the World Communist Party Congress, calls for a wide range of antiwar activities, the main features of which are for the people of the free world to urge the abolition of foreign bases and to fight militarization of their own countries, particularly against the alleged revanchism of West German and Japanese militarism.

It calls for a wide united front and strengthening of positive action of the masses. The united front is one of the most important tactics of Communist movements and proposes a wide range of alliances of all antigovernment forces. United front tactics are best described in the talk Mao Tse-tung had with a visiting group of Japanese Socialists in 1961. Mao said:

The inside of the Japanese government is dis-arranged; there are so-called main-stream factions and anti-main-stream factions and they are divided. For you the Chinese people are direct allies. The contradiction within the Liberal-Democratic Party is an indirect ally. Is it not true? . . . It is in the interest of the people that their split be widened and the two factions have mutual conflict and fight.

In its effort to gain wider support for the policy objective of the Communist party and to support the mass movements for it, the front organizations are very important. Front organizations of the international Communist movement, such as the World Peace Council or the World Labor Federation, keep close contact not only with its suborgans but with many leftist or labor organizations of various countries. In Japan, as well, some organizations which are not always under the direct leadership of international communism send delegations to these congresses and quite often decide to respect the decisions adopted there for their activities in Japan.

It is hard to determine to what degree various Japanese antiwar movements have been under the direct or indirect influence of the international Communist movement. It is undeniable, however, that their themes for struggle, sometimes antinuclear arms, sometimes antiforeign bases, sometimes anti-San Francisco peace treaty, sometimes anti-Vietnam war, reflect to a large degree the main theme proposed by Soviet-sponsored international Communist movements at each period.

Now let us turn to the basic meaning of these struggles. According to the official Russian explanation, as quoted above, these movements are meant to avoid world war through antiwar action by concentrating the energy of all "democratic peace-loving forces." Soviet Russia itself knows very well that peaceful coexistence is based on the East-West nuclear balance and not at all on the antiwar movement. Therefore the Soviet intention must lie somewhere else, quite conceivably not for attaining peaceful coexistence, but on the contrary for promoting its struggle against the West favorably under the given condition of peaceful coexistence. This is well shown in the following speech of Khrushchev in January of 1961:

The policy to fight positively for peace is making socialist foreign policy action a dynamic one. In these years the initiative in the international scene is taken always by the Soviet Union and socialist countries. Imperialist states and their governments are always on the defensive. Their prestige has declined to an unprecedented degree. The principle of peaceful co-existence helps the growth of the forces which are fighting for progress and socialism.

The struggle for defending peace as a Soviet policy doctrine existed even before Khrushchev's time. It was incorporated into the entire structure of peaceful coexistence. After Khrushchev and after the lapse of peaceful coexistence, the peace movement survives as before in the form of the antiwar, anti-Vietnam campaigns.

We must be aware that political propaganda and united front tactics will remain as long as the Leninist Communist movement exists. The peace offensive will survive peaceful coexistence or detente. There is no difference between the USSR and China on this point.

Struggle for People's Liberation

In sum, the principle of peaceful coexistence is not applied to the struggles for people's liberation. This conclusion is clearer in Chinese theory than in the Soviet and clearer in Brezhnev's than in Khrushchev's, but what they mean, whether in clear or ambiguous language, is practically the same.

As an example of the Soviet pattern of thought, consider *The Communist*, June 1963:

Peaceful co-existence does not mean abandonment of the severe ideological struggle. ... The implementation of the peaceful co-existence policy by Russia and other socialist countries is itself a campaign against imperialist designs to punish the people's liberation movement and is closely related to the defense of liberated countries against intrigues of world reactionaries ...

Also at the Twenty-third Party Congress Brezhnev made it clear that the principle of peaceful coexistence does not apply to relations between oppressors and the oppressed, or between colonialists and victims of colonial oppression. He also declared that the Soviet Party considers it as an international obligation to exert its utmost effort to support the struggles of nations for complete liberation from the oppression of colonialism and neocolonialism.

Three problems may be worth closer examination on the question of the struggle for people's liberation. They are: (1) definition of the people's liberation movement, which is quite often vague, (2) cases of the possible conflicts between the two principles of peaceful coexistence and the struggle for people's liberation, and (3) which of the two forces in newly emerging nations should be supported, the nationalist regime of the country or revolutionary elements within that country.

The first question has become a particularly complicated issue since Communists started using the term "neocolonialism." The Eighty-One Parties Congress in 1960 declares that "the imperialists are trying to maintain the colonial exploitation in a new form." According to this definition, the Western nations are gaining a new position under the name of "economic aid," inducing these newly independent nations into military blocs, forcing upon them dictatorial military regimes and building military bases in these countries. Moreover, it accuses Western nations of distorting the significance of self-determination and trying to achieve colonial domination under the pretext of mutual help.

This definition will apply to most Japanese actions in Southeast Asia in giving economic aid and strengthening the relation of mutual interdependence by enlarging trade relations. In fact, many nations in Southeast Asia friendly to Japan are non-Communist and quite a few of them have military regimes. If we accept the definition that it is neocolonialism to strengthen relations and exchanges with these countries, we will be prevented from trading or investing in the Asian region except in Communist countries. In sum, the Communist side can criticize any political or economic measures taken by the non-Communist countries in that region under the name of the struggle for people's liberation and against colonialism and neocolonialism. It would certainly be against the Japanese national interest, as well as the true interest of all countries in the region, to accommodate to their theory. We have to recognize that there still exists a line which we cannot possibly cross in accommodating proposals of Communist countries.

The term "struggle for people's liberation" is sometimes used in another loose way. For example, the Palestine question—the Arab-Israeli conflict—has been defined very often since 1966 as a struggle for people's liberation by Arabs against Israel in the language of both the Soviet Union and China. It implies a theoretical danger. Suppose, in a case of any racial conflict, a Communist side unilaterally defines one party as the victim of colonial oppression and the other as the oppressor, and suppose that the principle of the people's liberation movement has priority over that of peaceful coexistence, it implies the theoretical possibility of unlimited escalation. Of course, again, the reality is not so simple. We do not expect at this moment any real possibility of the Soviets or Chinese risking a nuclear war in supporting the Arab side in the Palestine question.

This directly leads to the second question: the conflict between the principle of peaceful coexistence and the people's liberation movement. The conflict will take place, as a possible practical example, if the people's liberation movement escalates into a civil war in which both ideological sides are deeply committed and if both sides seriously consider the use of nuclear weapons as the measure to win the war, even risking further escalation into a global war.

Theoretically speaking there is no problem. China admits that peaceful coexistence is no more than a tactic and that support for a people's liberation movement is a sacred duty of the socialist states. The priority is obvious. The Soviet attitude is the same.

However, practice would be obviously different. Rather, this may be offered as a marked example of the difference between Communist theory and practice. Full-scale war can decide the fate of a state and a nation. The only case where a country, including the USSR or China, decides to go to war is either that it believes it will win the war and be able to survive, or that it is faced with a real threat to its very existence as a sovereign nation, or as a system in which it believes. There is little possibility, even for China, in an intense or fanatical ideological period risking total nuclear warfare, however just it may appear under Lenin's definition, which is not directly related to China's own existence. In this sense there is no difference between avoiding a nuclear war as a tactic or as the fundamental principle of peaceful coexistence.

So far we have examined the extreme case. Of course there could be many variations in a people's liberation movement. Usually circumstances in Asia are better suited than in Europe for people's liberation movements, and likewise for any local conflicts to take place without the risk of developing into nuclear wars. The comparatively radical attitude of China may be explained by this circumstance. China can afford to be more radical.

A third question is rather a question between the USSR and China, and does not really concern us. Therefore the analysis will be very brief. According to Communist theory, the proletariat is still weak as a force in Afro-Asian countries and therefore it is often useful to support a nationalist bourgeoisie in such circumstances. China insists that support of a nationalist bourgeoisie does not go far enough in these countries which have already achieved independence. This dispute has a deep root. In the long struggle of the Chinese Communist party through the Sino-Japanese war and the civil war, the USSR never decided to give exclusive support to the Chinese Communist party. The Chinese Communist party leaders must remember many events in which they believed that they suffered damage because of the lack of support from the Soviets. In the

Sino-Indian border incident, which was one of the decisive turning points in Sino-Soviet relations, Soviet support was obviously behind the nationalist bourgeois regime of Nehru. In the period after the Sino-Indian border incident, and all through the cultural revolution, the USSR endeavored to normalize its relations with Southeast Asian nationalist states, while China concentrated its efforts more or less on support for the people's liberation movements in these countries.

However, it is again doubtful if this is a conflict between principles. The nationalist regime of Pakistan was almost the only friend of China in Asia in that period and the Chinese never openly or perhaps not even tacitly supported the subversive activities of the Pakistan Communist party. The situation was more paradoxical in the case of Bangladesh, where Russia supported the self-determination of the Bengal people and China was opposed to it. Moreover, the Russian attitude in the case of Bangladesh was somewhat contradictory to that in the case of Biafra. Therefore, even this deep-rooted conflict of principle can be easily modified for convenience.

Every instance of Chinese reaction in the context of the people's liberation movement in various situations can be found in the Vietnam conflict between 1965-1973. We can safely assume, with some evidence, that China was prepared for possible confrontation with the United States at certain stages. Their assistance to the people's liberation movement of Vietnam must have been cautiously measured against possible U.S. reactions. Many people believe that the Chinese would have intervened in case the existence of North Vietnam as a state had been seriously threatened, just as they did in Korea. Although this hypothesis remained unproved, the Chinese leadership must have breathed a sign of relief when it became clear that the chance of U.S.-Chinese confrontation over Vietnam had passed.

It appears that the steam is somewhat out of the people's liberation movement in Asia after the Vietnam war, which was thought to be one of its highest forms. Worsening of Sino-Soviet relations, which led China to shift the weight of its external policy from "revolutionary diplomacy" to more normal relations with the U.S. and Japan, may have contributed to this. It is hard to predict at this stage the future of the Chinese policy on people's liberation movement.

Sino-Soviet Polemics

In the previous section, we examined the Chinese position on peaceful coexistence in the period of Sino-Soviet polemics. I think it convenient to define this period chronologically as the ten years between 1956 to 1965. In the late 1950s the polemics were not quite visible to outsiders. Only by looking back to Chinese documents of the late 1950s, after the Sino-Soviet disputes had become obvious in the early 1960s, did most people find out that the Sino-Soviet polemics started right after the Twentieth Soviet Party Congress in 1956. After 1966, the Sino-Soviet confrontation became more one of state-to-state antagonism than of ideological disputes. At least it became rather difficult to find Soviet or Chinese statements worth quoting after 1966 to explain the theoretical evolution of the polemics. In polemics two parties are supposed to have different views and say different things. The Soviets and Chinese did say different things prior to 1966, but since then the Chinese have called the Russians imperialistic and antirevolutionary and the Russians have called the Chinese imperialistic and antirevolutionary; the Chinese accused the Russians of connivance with the United States and the Russians accused the Chinese of connivance with the United States; and so on.

We have seen that in those ten years, the Chinese attitude was more loyal to the traditional interpretation of Marxism-Leninism, in other words, more doctrinaire and more inflexible. It also put more emphasis on the struggle of the people's liberation movement than on peaceful coexistence. So far as rhetoric is concerned this is still their basic attitude. However, prior to the ten years, from 1954 to 1956, there was a period of so-called "Bandung diplomacy," and again quite recently China is showing a more flexible attitude in practice though not necessarily in words. Therefore it may be worthwhile to look into the period prior to the Sino-Soviet polemics for a key to other potential Chinese policies.

Bandung Diplomacy

The term "Bandung diplomacy" refers to the comparatively flexible Chinese external policy shown in the period after Stalin's death and the Korean truce, which culminated in the Afro-Asian Conference in Bandung in 1955. When I wrote the Japanese edition of this book I paid particular attention to this period because, as I wrote, the flexible Chinese attitude of this period might suggest a possibility to be borne in mind in connection with the future improvement of Sino-Japanese relations. On many points the Chinese have recently returned to their attitude of the Bandung period and made Sino-Japanese normalization much easier than expected. Therefore the policy implication elaborated in this chapter has at least been partly borne out. Analysis of this period is, however, still useful, partly because it allows a comparative study of present Chinese policy and of that prior to the period of Sino-Soviet polemics, and partly because it might give a clue to the durability of the present flexible attitude.

How flexible was China in 1955? I quote from the speech given at the Bandung Conference by Chou En-lai:

Peaceful coexistence between nations of different social systems will be made possible by upholding the principles of respect for sovereignty, security for territorial integrity, non-aggression, non-intervention in domestic affairs, equality and mutual benefits among nations. I see no reason why international disputes cannot be solved by negotiation if these principles will be implemented.

These are the so-called five principles of peace proposed by China. They were first embodied in the Sino-Indian Treaty of 1954.

These principles are further explained in the same speech.

If nations promise each other not to conduct aggression, an international environment for peaceful coexistence will be achieved. If they promise not to intervene in domestic affairs of other countries, each nation can freely choose its own political system and its way of life.

These principles were reiterated by Chou at the meeting of the Standing Committee of the National People's Congress on May 13, 1955:

The principles underlying the foreign policy of the People's Republic of China are the defense of its national independence, sovereign freedom, rights, and territorial integrity, supporting a lasting international peace and friendly cooperation among the people of all countries, and opposition to the imperialist policy of aggression and war. These principles are at one with the common desires and demands of the peoples of the Asian and African countries.

The striking difference between the above statement and the Chinese attitude during the Sino-Soviet polemics explained in the previous section is self-evident. They are theoretically two different attitudes. For example, as soon as China declared that peaceful coexistence cannot be a fundamental policy, the validity of the five principles became theoretically very limited. If support for people's liberation movements has priority over nonintervention in domestic affairs, the principle of nonintervention becomes meaningless. China is free to call upon people in other countries to stand up for a revolution, which already constitutes a violation of the principle, and to support these revolutionary movements if China judges that the support is requested by these revolutionaries. In fact, there are many such instances in the latter half of the 1960s.

In fact the importance of the five principles gradually declined all through the 1960s. Particularly in the latter half of the 1960s, the five principles were rarely quoted in any communiques between China and other countries with one or two exceptions, as far as I remember, during the period of the cultural revolution, while these principles were ubiquitously quoted in the middle of the 1950s.

A remarkable example of gradual decay is found in China's relations with India, with whom Chou En-lai declared the five principles for the first time in 1954. The *People's Daily* of December 21, 1963 said, "We have consistently maintained the policy of strengthening and developing peaceful co-existence and friendly cooperation with countries of Asia, Africa and Latin America. At the same time we are executing a necessary struggle against a country which violates the five principles and destroys them, like India." Thus India was excluded from the application of peaceful coexistence. China did not think any longer that "no problem is insoluble by negotiations" with India.

The attitude toward Japan has also changed. The Sino-Japanese question in the postwar period has always been boiled down to Japanese relations with Taiwan. Therefore the Chinese attitude toward Japanese policy on Taiwan serves as a yardstick for measuring Chinese flexibility toward Japan.

The margin of Chinese flexibility is not so large. It may appear ridiculously small to outsiders, but it has made a substantial difference in Sino-Japanese relations and Japanese politics concerning the China question. In Japan this question has been a major factor dividing public opinion, as the Vietnam question was in the United States. On August 17, 1955, a visiting Japanese team from the mass media asked Chou En-lai whether they were supposed to understand that the abolition of the Japanese-Taiwan Treaty is not a prerequisite for normalizing the Sino-Japanese relation, but is an objective to be achieved eventually as the result of working toward Sino-Japanese normalization. Chou answered "Yes, generally." A further elaboration of this position may be seen in Chou En-lai's talks with Japanese reporters on July 25, 1957. He said

At this moment the relations between China and Japan are not yet normalized. The state of war continues under international law. This fact, however, does not prevent both nations from having friendly relations and from concluding non-governmental agreements.

By greatly promoting this kind of Sino-Japanese relations, eventually the end of the state of war will be declared according to diplomatic practice and normal relations will be established.

This attitude allowed Japan to execute the so-called "policy of separating political affairs from economic affairs." It meant that Japan could expand trade and other relations with China while maintaining diplomatic relations with Taiwan at least for the moment. This Chinese attitude was sharply changed following the so-called Nagasaki flag incident in 1958.[e] In subsequent years the volume of trade was cut drastically. Although trade recovered, as Sino-Soviet economic relations deteriorated in the early 1960s, the Chinese position in principle remained rigid for ten years until a few months before Prime Minister Tanaka's visit to Peking. In these ten years China was categorically opposed to the idea of separating political affairs from economic affairs and also urged

[e]This was a case in which a young Japanese man pulled down a PRC flag at a show of Chinese stamps, brocades, and paperwork at a department store in Nagasaki on May 2, 1958. The man was arrested on the charge of offense against property. On May 9 Chinese Foreign Minister Cheng criticized the Japanese government for failing to try him on the charge of offense against a foreign flag and on May 11 he announced the rupture of all economic and cultural ties with Japan.

acceptance beforehand of the Chinese position on Taiwan, which was expressed in the so-called three principles of Sino-Japanese normalization.[f] The result of the negotiations during the Tanaka visit in 1972 was very much in line with Chou's position in 1956. Both parties started the negotiations without any preconditions, and after Sino-Japanese relations were thus normalized, diplomatic relations with Taiwan were eventually severed by Japan. Nonetheless, Japan continued to maintain very extensive relations with Taiwan, except diplomatic relations.

Therefore, so far as Sino-Japanese relations are concerned, one could say that the Chinese attitude somewhat resembles their attitude during the Bandung diplomacy. In order to see, however, if the flexible attitude of recent Chinese diplomacy is really following the pattern of Bandung diplomacy, we must look more closely into the matter in relation to Chinese policy toward the United States.

It is not easy to find a good quotation of Chinese policy of peaceful coexistence toward the United States even at the peak of the Bandung diplomacy. One of the rare examples I could quote is the report of Liu Shao-chi in September 1956. It said "The policy of peaceful coexistence is spread over relations with all countries. We are prepared to apply this policy (even) to the United States." The United States is mentioned here as a logical consequence of saying "all countries." Particular note of the United States is restricted to the phrase "(even) to the United States," meaning the last country to which to apply the principle. The meaning is further diluted by saying "prepared to." It is also noteworthy that it is hard to find quotations of Mao or Chou proposing peaceful coexistence with the United States in that period.

Most of the time the Chinese principle of peaceful coexistence is applied to countries of "Asia, Africa and Latin America," or to "all peace-loving nations." The Chinese idea becomes clearer in the theory of the so-called *intermediary zone.* The theory says that the world can be divided into three zones: A Socialist zone, a capitalist zone, and an intermediary zone of independent Asian, African, and Latin American states, and that the Socialist zone and the intermediary zone should unite in their struggles against imperialism. The theory includes such variations as enlarging and dividing the intermediary zone into two categories of advanced and less-advanced countries, or proposing the tactics of all the "countryside of the world" to besiege all the "cities of the world," obviously taking after the victorious tactics of the Chinese revolution.

One of my most respected teachers of Chinese Communist affairs, who died a few years ago, said, when he was asked what he would consider the single most important philosophy of Mao Tse-tung, "to make a distinction between enemy and allies." According to him Mao defines the enemy in the narrowest sense and

---

[f]The so-called three principles demanded that Japan recognize: (1) the PRC as the sole legal government of China, (2) Taiwan as an inalienable part of the PRC, and (3) the Japan-PRC Peace Treaty as unlawful, invalid, and to be denounced. These principles were often presented as prerequisite for the Sino-Japanese normalization.

considers all those who do not belong to the enemy to be allies. We can safely say that until very recently the United States was considered the enemy of China. Mao tried to organize a united front against the United States. That united front included all Asian, African, and Latin American countries, and sometimes even more advanced Western nations. It was a policy of isolating the United States.

Here is the fundamental difference between the Soviet notion of peaceful coexistence and that of China, at least until 1970. Soviet peaceful coexistence starts from relations with its principal enemy, the United States. It appears that in the USSR peaceful coexistence is a relation exclusively applied to the United States. Peaceful relations with other countries is another matter. The Chinese theory is, on the contrary, that peaceful coexistence applies to all countries other than the United States and is designed to isolate the principal enemy. Of course the difference was born out of circumstances and necessity. The Soviet Union does not have another alternative in the face of the possibility of a totally destructive nuclear confrontation with the United States. On the other hand the Chinese theory was more abstract. While considering the United States as the principal enemy, which seized the Chinese territory of Taiwan, China did not possess sufficient physical power to overwhelm the United States. The only possible way was to propose an international united front against it. Contradictorily, however, the period in which the Chinese proposed the united front strategy against the United States was also a doctrinaire and inflexible period of Chinese diplomacy. In that period China lost its friends because of its emphasis on people's liberation movements in those countries and its extremely inflexible diplomacy during the cultural revolution, and it was rather China which was isolated in the international scene.

From the above analysis it is hard to say that the recent flexible attitude of China is somewhat similar to that in the middle of the 1950s. In the 1950s the United States was the principal enemy and Chinese diplomacy was flexible enough to improve its relation with all countries except the United States. Therefore we have to assume something quite new has happened. Although I do not intend to go very much beyond the scope of my book as originally written (and also because it is still imprudent to define the present world situation), at least we can assume that the United States is no longer the principal enemy of China. This means, according to Mao's strategical philosophy, that the United States is viewed as an ally, since any country which is not the principal enemy should be an ally. And there is a principal enemy of China somewhere else. I stop here, but I might note that in my original book, while stating a pessimistic view on the future of Chinese attitudes toward the West, I made two reservations for optimism: the possible effect of Sino-Soviet tension and the possibility of China departing from Maoist philosophy.

This reflection also explains the difference between Sino-Japanese relations and Sino-American relations. Japan, although very often criticized by China as imperialist or militarist, has never been the principal enemy of China in the postwar period. Therefore, it was a potential friend of China in the second intermediary zone, the zone of advanced countries, for the purpose of a united front to isolate the United States. Also, at present Japan is clearly not the principal enemy of China and could be counted as a possible ally. In that sense Chinese strategy toward Japan has not changed and therefore we can find a similarity between the flexible Chinese attitude of the middle 1950s and that of the present time. In the case of the United States it is important to bear in mind that this is a new situation, although quite explainable on the basis of Mao's doctrine and philosophy.

Some Thoughts on the Vicissitudes
of Chinese Policy

In the original Japanese version this section was written with the possibility always in mind that the Chinese attitude might return to the flexible one of the mid-1950s, in other words with the possibility of improvement in Sino-Japanese relations. Although this policy implication is superseded by the recent Sino-Japanese normalization, I think it still useful to preserve this chapter, particularly in order to provide some clues in our effort to forsee the future course of Chinese foreign policy.

There exists a tendency to explain the cycle of Chinese foreign policy changes by the external conditions surrounding China. The policy implication of this theory is that our attitude toward China, either soft or tough, will affect Chinese foreign policy, therefore the inflexible attitude of China is at least partly our fault.

It is not difficult to prove this theory. It can be done simply by following the line of the Chinese official explanation. The Chinese flexible attitude toward Japan in 1955-56 is explained by the fact that the Hatoyama and Ishibashi cabinets were more friendly toward China than the preceding Yoshida cabinet or succeeding Kishi cabinet. The Chinese explain the suspension of "the Memorandum Trade" in 1958 by Chinese unilateral action by averring that the Japanese government did not show a sincere attitude toward the friendly measures the Chinese had extended to Japan in the preceding period. The Memorandum Trade under a new name, LT Trade, was reopened because the Japanese representative was a respectable member of the governing Liberal Democratic party and gradual political improvement was expected, and because friendly relations between the Japanese and Chinese people would be strengthened in spite of the abortive effort of a minority to hinder it. The "severe" Chinese attitude toward the Sato cabinet was explained by the "reactionary" nature of the Sato cabinet.

Let us leave Sino-Japanese relations for a moment and look objectively at

Chinese politics in both the Chinese domestic policy aspect and the global strategy aspect.

In the period between 1954 and 1956 Chinese diplomacy showed its most flexible pattern, keeping pace with Khrushchevian peaceful coexistence, as we have already seen. In 1954 China was represented at the Geneva Conference for peace in Indochina. In April 1954 Chou and Nehru declared the five principles of peaceful coexistence, which were reconfirmed in an expanded form in the Bandung Conference in April 1955. In August 1955 the marathon Sino-American ambassadorial talks started.

Assessment of domestic policy is more delicate. Certainly there was no particular emphasis put on revolutionary idealism and regimentation such as in the preceding period of the "Three-Antis" and the "Five-Antis" or in the succeeding period of the "Great Leap." In that sense it was a moderate period. There was also the period of the "Hundred Flowers" in 1956. Assessment of this "Hundred Flower" movement is divided. Although a short period of literary freedom existed, it was followed by harsh measures which cut the blossoms which had bloomed. Some observers believe this relaxation followed by a purge was a premeditated move. At any rate this period coincided with that of the Chinese flexible attitude toward Japan during the Hatoyama Cabinet.

In 1957 the doctrinaire attitude of China surfaced through Sino-Soviet polemics. In 1958 the policy of the Great Leap was adopted and the People's Commune initiated. In August of that year China started large-scale bombardment of Quemoy and Matsu. In Sino-Japanese relations China decided to cut the "Memorandum Trade" relation on the occasion of the Nagasaki flag incident in May 1958 and then intensified its campaign against revision of the U.S.-Japan security treaty in the years around 1960.

From the beginning of the 1960s the Chinese economy suffered severely from the failure of the Great Leap policy, according to the official Chinese explanation because of bad weather, and by the dwindling of Sino-Soviet trade as their relations deteriorated. Since 1961-1962, China's main trade shifted from the countries of the Communist bloc to the advanced Western nations. With Japan it started the "LT trade." The volume of the Sino-Japanese trade has grown since then at a tremendous pace. On the domestic side a relatively moderate attitude was maintained and a partial recovery of even literary freedom (or covert anti-Mao expression) was noticed.

As economic stability was regained the Chinese attitude showed again a change toward more revolutionary idealism—externally in 1965 and internally in 1966—and then plunged into the extremist period of the cultural revolution. Its relations with foreign countries hit bottom in that period. With Japan, while its stand involving major principles stiffened and the war of words was escalated, trade volume itself was unaffected.

Now how important was the influence of the Japanese attitude on these Chinese transitions? It is presumptuous to believe that the Hatoyama and

Ishibashi Cabinets induced a flexible attitude in China in the years 1954-56. That flexibility was clearly global in character and not limited with respect to Japan.

What was the reason for the sudden disruption of economic and cultural relations with Japan in 1958? The official reason given by China was that the Japanese government failed to give legal protection to the flag of the People's Republic of China under the law covering disrespect toward foreign flags. Because Japan did not at that time recognize the People's Republic of China, such protection could only be offered under the law to protect property in general. Since this was so, the resumption of trade relations in 1962 was obviously contradictory. Not only on this particular aspect of the legal protection of the national flag, but on all other related aspects covering Sino-Japanese relations, the conditions were practically the same in 1958 and 1962 and on, until 1972. Suspecting other reasons behind all this, one should certainly take note that already, prior to the incident, China seemed to have decided to launch radical domestic policies and to assert a more doctrinaire attitude toward the outside world.

The reasons given for the resumption of the Memorandum Trade in 1962 are full of contradictions, as we have seen above. The real reason must have been the sharp decline in China's economic relations with the Soviet Union. Actually, China increased her trade with all advanced Western nations, not only with Japan.

The tremendous expansion of Sino-Japanese trade during the long years of the Sato Cabinet may not be connected with the attitude of the Japanese government. In this period the Japanese government departed from the so-called low posture policy of the Ikeda Cabinet, which had meant avoiding confrontation with leftist forces domestically and internationally, and consolidated its cooperative relations with the free world by concluding the Japanese-Korean Treaty and by achieving the Okinawa Reversion. This latter achievement must not have been welcomed by China, considering Chinese policy during that period. Apart from economic relations, the hardening of the Chinese attitude toward Japan in word and gesture was quite noticeable between 1966 and 1970. Here again this hardening was general and not limited to Japan. It was really global, affecting the Soviet Union, Great Britain, whose embassy was mobbed and set afire, India, Burma, Indonesia, etc., and of course the United States. It is far easier to explain the change in Chinese attitudes by the rise and fall of the cultural revolution than by the reactionary tendency of the Sato Cabinet.

The inevitable conclusion is that in deciding its foreign policy, domestic motives have been far more important than the external environment for China, and much more so in China than in other countries. Therefore, it is dangerous to assume that China will change its attitude if we change our attitude.

After all these analyses, what is the importance of Japan to China? We have seen that in China domestic elements are more important than external elements in decisions affecting its foreign policy. Among these external elements, its relations with the Soviet Union and the United States must have overwhelming importance. Therefore we must admit that other external elements have only limited influence on China. But the importance of Japan to China, however limited it is, may be next to that of these two superpowers. Japan is the third biggest industrial power after the United States and the Soviet Union. In the circumstance where trade with the Soviet Union has been drastically reduced and trade with the United States is still very small, China must give importance to the technology and products which Japan can provide. Geographical proximity must also be considered as an advantage in connection with trade. Politically, Japan has had very close relations with Korea and Taiwan, which have been sensitive areas also for China. Moreover, since the memories of the past war still linger, China would never underestimate the potential threat of Japan, and even appears to commit the mistake of overestimation.

Judging from Chinese comments on Japan, it appears as if the Chinese attitude toward Japan vacillates between the expectation that Japan, with such economic and political importance, will desert the orbit of American world strategy and thus contribute to the Chinese interest in the Far East, and the nightmare of the revival of Japanese militarism. Various opinions expressed in the open and pluralistic Japanese society may have contributed to the above Chinese expectation and fear.

What is necessary for a more stable Sino-Japanese relationship is to make Chinese leaders understand that, in spite of various opinions expressed in a pluralistic Japanese society, the system of democracy and cooperation with the free world are very deeply imbedded in the Japanese people. China is expected to understand that the free and democratic society of Japan will never change toward militarism and also that a firm belief in democracy rules out the possibility of Japan's drifting from cooperation with the United States and other free nations. A stable relation should be built upon the foundation of these understandings. Perhaps China understands this already, but it still maneuvers to achieve an anti-American united front. If so, China should understand that the Japanese people will react adversely to such maneuvers, and that they are harmful to real friendship between China and Japan. The Japanese side too should be careful to avoid giving any false image of Japan to China. A relationship won by giving China a false expectation or by ingratiating oneself in agreeing with Chinese fears, not necessarily out of one's own belief, will certainly fail. A genuine friendship will be born only by conveying to the other party a correct assessment and the clear intentions of the party.

3

Detente Diplomacy

From Peaceful Coexistence to Detente Diplomacy

As previously pointed out, detente diplomacy is one of the vaguest terms of contemporary international affairs. It is sometimes intentionally vague, sometimes essentially vague and sometimes nonexistent as a technical term which possesses a definite meaning. As a nonacademic, I do not intend to define it, but simply try to illustrate what was called "detente diplomacy" in the latter half of the 1960s and to find out what was, as philosophy, lying behind the so-called detente diplomacy.

In order better to understand the overall picture, however, I will try to sort out schools of thinking on detente or detente policy in the 1960s. Generally speaking, there are two major schools of thought on this problem. One school thinks that the policy of peaceful coexistence and detente policy are one thing seen from different angles and should not be artificially differentiated, or believes there is no such thing as detente diplomacy. The other thought notes that peaceful coexistence was deliberately initiated by the Communist side and detente diplomacy by the Western side, and tries to find out the inevitable historical difference in these two approaches. This second approach deals with the strategic interaction between the Communist approach to politics as class struggle and the West. In this book I rather followed the second approach for convenience of factual study, but theoretically I am not necessarily committed to either of them.

A School of Thought Which Does Not Believe in Detente Policy As Such

This way of thinking accommodates common sense in international affairs, but at the same time is supported by the strict theoretical way of thinking of the Soviet Union.

According to common sense, peaceful coexistence means a friendly and peaceful relation between states of different political systems and East-West detente means a relaxation of tension between such states. Therefore, peaceful coexistence should be basic to East-West detente and East-West detente is a good thing for maintaining and strengthening peaceful coexistence.

43

In that case, detente policy can comprise a very wide range of diplomatic activities. It may include all diplomatic activities except one based on the threat or use of force. As long as there exist nations and states in this world and they have contact with one another, since no country can isolate itself completely from others, it is inevitable that they have conflicting interests. These conflicting interests create international frictions and tensions. We must recognize the fact that frictions and tensions are inevitable between sovereign states and that, although it is possible to minimize frictions by mutual compromise, complete elimination of tensions is possible only when one country gives up its national interest in order to accommodate that of the others. It appears sometimes that a state of no friction is achieved between a big power and its satellite state, or between a colonial power and its colony. Obviously the unequal status of the parties must make it possible.

Detente policy in the broadest sense may be defined as a policy meant to minimize the friction or tension which is inevitable among sovereign nations. It includes not only traditional good neighbor diplomacy, but also all diplomatic activities which regulate bilateral business, cultural activities which promote mutual understanding of nations, economic aid activities aimed at alleviating the North-South economic difference, UN diplomacy for a long-term organization of international society and even protocolar affairs among states. In other words, detente diplomacy in this sense is that diplomacy which every nation practices in peace time. Therefore there is no such thing as detente diplomacy.

The Soviet concept is not exactly the same, but nevertheless somewhat similar. Brezhnevian definition of peaceful coexistence is much narrower than that of common sense: Peaceful coexistence is the will of the Soviet Union and the United States to avoid a nuclear war, and perhaps nothing else. It is doubtful even whether the peaceful relations between nonnuclear states of different systems could be called peaceful coexistence under the Russian theory.

Russians do not use the word "detente policy." The word detente is used mainly on two occasions. The most numerous instances may be seen where the Soviet Union attacks actions of Western countries, and recently that of China, as being against detente. The other occasion is where it emphasizes an achievement made by the Soviet Union, particularly in its effort to regulate relations with the West, as a contribution to detente. In any case detente is a description of a state achieved or affected. There is no such thing as "detente policy" in Soviet terminology. The Soviets are particularly wary of "detente policy," which implies a gradual convergence of their system and another, and thus a compromise between the two worlds, as will be explained in a later chapter.

An Approach to Differentiate Detente
Policy as a Separate Entity from
Peaceful Coexistence

If there is any such thing as detente policy, it consists of the entire policy of the Western side toward the Communist world in the latter half of the 1960s and the

1970s under the rubric of "detente policy." The question is how to differentiate it from the Soviet policy of "peaceful coexistence."

Here let us once again examine different concepts of East-West relations which appeared in the 1960s.

1. The strictest interpretation of peaceful coexistence is, as repeatedly explained, no more than the other aspect of nuclear deterrence. Therefore, it is a policy which can be implemented only by powers who are capable of overall nuclear warfare. Various moves for peaceful coexistence and detente in Europe are entirely within the framework of U.S.-USSR peaceful coexistence. All these moves can be prompted as long as both the United States and the USSR approve them, but stop where one of these superpowers refuses to accept them.

The present Soviet definition runs somewhat along this line. Some Westerners who are determined not to have any illusions about Soviet intentions are likewise very careful to define present East-West relations as being nothing more than this Soviet understanding. Of course there exist many other aspects of relations between the United States and the Soviet Union, but, in this narrowly defined sense, they do not fall within the framework of the relation of peaceful coexistence but belong to normal bilateral relations in the traditional sense of power politics.

Although it sounds paradoxical, according to this school of thought, detente policy may mean power politics. At least both detente policy and power politics are antitheses of the ideological confrontation of the cold war type. In fact, if the recent American detente with the Soviet Union and China is the direct result of Sino-Soviet tension, there is very little practical difference in saying that the United States is conducting a detente policy with the USSR and China, or engaging in power politics with the Soviet Union and China.

2. Remaining loyal to the narrowest interpretation as explained above, application of peaceful coexistence can be substantially enlarged. To avoid a nuclear war requires eliminating causes for generating a nuclear confrontation. If so, all the efforts to eliminate both distant and immediate causes of a nuclear confrontation fall in the category of the policy of peaceful coexistence. Tacit or explicit understanding between the United States and the USSR on the Middle East may be said to be based on the policy of peaceful coexistence, in the sense that it is avoiding a nuclear war which might start in that area. According to some observers, German acquiescence in the semi-permanent division of Germany was achieved by the determination of the United States and the USSR not to risk war on the European front.

Some people use the word detente to describe both the policy and its result in these instances. One may say, however, that this kind of policy will quite safely fall under the Soviet definition of peaceful coexistence, however narrow this may be, and not constitute an example of detente policy separate from the policy of peaceful coexistence.

3. Sometimes the policy of peaceful coexistence goes beyond the basic definition of merely avoiding a nuclear confrontation. Though I do not repeat them here, there could be many quotations from what Khrushchev and Chou

have said in the period 1954-1956. They stress not only the various measures to achieve strategic balance but also economic and cultural exchanges to promote mutual understanding, friendship, and cooperation between the states of different systems. One might call it the maximum point ever reached under the name of peaceful coexistence. Or since it is different from the current Communist definition of peaceful coexistence, one might call it something else which has gone beyond the bounds of peaceful coexistence and, therefore, call it propaganda or detente policy, according to how one perceives it.

4. Detente policy, as professed and executed by the Western nations in the latter half of the 60s, also proposed the peaceful settlement of disputes and promoted various East-West exchanges. In that sense it appears almost the same as peaceful coexistence, reaching its maximum, as shown in the preceding paragraph. Some might say that the same approach is called peaceful coexistence by the East and detente policy by the West, irrespective of which side initiates it. If there is any difference, it is in its policy implication. Detente policy, in a very discreet way and in a careful expression, suggests, in addition to the basic purpose of maintaining peace, some changes in the status quo of East-West relations and the possibility of a solution of outstanding East-West problems in the long run through these changes. It appears to advocate peace and then hopes that the peace itself will create more long-lasting effects on the societies on both sides of the East-West dividing line, and thus change long-term political prospects. The true policy implication of detente policy is always ambiguous. The Russian side ignores its policy implication as long as it is vague, but reacts strongly against it when the implications become more explicit.

Detente Policy

In the analysis of the so-called detente policy by Western nations I put special emphasis on the year 1966. Of course the condition of detente has prevailed many times in the postwar period, starting with the "thaw" after Stalin's death, until the current "age of dialogue." I think, however, that the atmosphere in the late 1960s was unique, unique in the sense that people were both serious and optimistic. Then, they seriously and squarely faced ideological problems and the question of the future of the two systems, distinctly different from the current attitude of leaving ideology in abeyance. Moreover, they were idealistic and optimistic, again in contrast with the current mood of cynical realism. The attitudes both in 1966 and now can be legitimately called detente policy, but the mood of the two periods is completely different.

The following epoch-making events marked the year 1966. In March the West German government produced the so-called Peace Note, which gave priority to the policy of detente and suggested a new course of German diplomacy for coming years even up to the present. In October the United States, which had always maintained the primary role in Western defense, declared in President Johnson's speech the policy of solving European problems by improving the East-West environment. And the NATO Ministerial Council meetings at the end of the year officially confirmed detente as an aim of NATO. Therefore, we can safely define the year 1966 as the time in which detente was first adopted as the common official policy of Western nations in the postwar period. Moreover, the year was marked by the symbolic event of General De Gaulle's visit to Moscow, the culminating act of his philosophy of "From the Atlantic to the Urals."

It was felt the peace or peaceful coexistence in Europe, which has been maintained twenty years and reassured by events in the early 1960s, had finally touched off the flowering of the East-West detente.

President Johnson's Concept of European
Detente and NATO Communique

In his speech on October 7, 1966 in New York, President Johnson set forth his concept of detente policy. He said, "Europe has been at peace since 1945. But it is a restless peace shadowed by the threat of violence." He later elaborated this point, stating that "Our task is to achieve a reconciliation with the East—a shift from the narrow concept of peaceful co-existence to the broader vision of peaceful engagement."[a] Here he clearly proposed a policy which could be called a detente policy and which is somewhat different from and somewhat beyond peaceful coexistence. The President recognized that the heart of the European problem was the German question, saying that

One great goal of a united West is to heal the wound in Europe which now cuts East from West and brother from brother. That division must be healed peacefully. It must be healed with the consent of Eastern European countries and the Soviet Union. This will happen only as East and West succeed in building a surer foundation of mutual trust. Nothing is more important for peace. We must improve the East-West environment in order to achieve the unification of Germany in the context of a larger peaceful and prosperous Europe.

A broader policy objective was set out as follows:

Our purpose is not to overturn other governments, but to help the people of Europe to achieve: a continent in which the peoples of Eastern and Western Europe work together for the common good; a continent in which alliances do not confront each other in bitter hostility, but provide a framework in which West and East can act together to assure the security of all. In a restored Europe, Germany can and will be united . . .

---

[a]This concept can be traced to the article by Z. Brzezinski and W.E. Griffith, "Peaceful Engagement in Europe's Future," *Foreign Affairs*, July 1961.

The idea of a solution in a "European framework" was also in fashion at that time. Originally it was a Gaullist notion. In addition to innumerable paragraphs in De Gaulle's memoirs, advancing this idea, the Soviet-French Declaration on June 30, 1966 at Moscow said that:

Both governments agree that the problems of Europe should be first of all discussed within European limits. They believe that the states of the continent should exert efforts to create conditions necessary for the establishment of an atmosphere of detente between all countries of the West and East since such an atmosphere would facilitate rapprochement and accord between them and, thus the discussion and settlement of arising problems.

It is an historical perspective, or, a long-term perspective beyond ideology. In the age of ideology, however, its implication is complex. It suggests the superiority of the common heritage of European civilization to ideology. In effect, it was calling upon East European countries to replace the East-West dividing line with the common heritage and pride of Europe. The ideological erosion of Marxism-Leninism, the politics of nationalism, not class struggle, might lead to the loosening of the solidarity of the Socialist camp. It also appealed to anti-American nationalism in West Europe, which in turn might tend to create anti-Russian nationalism in East Europe.

It is also worth noting that President Johnson said, "The division must be healed with the consent of Eastern European countries and the Soviet Union." This was before the Czechoslovakian invasion and the Brezhnev doctrine. It was a period in which people believed that East European nations were increasingly independent and could be induced to become still more independent from the Russians. In fact German Ostpolitik first dreamt of beginning detente with East Europeans with the conscious or unconscious effect of isolating East Germany, given the prevailing mood of detente. There was even a movement of "detente among small European nations" both from Eastern and Western sides. But as it turned out to be an illusion, the concept of U.S.-Soviet peaceful coexistence was gradually to re-emerge.

The most significant part of the speech is, of course, that it recognized that "that division must be healed *peacefully*. It must be healed with *the consent* of Eastern European countries and the Soviet Union," a clear renunciation of force as a means of achieving a united Germany. This was made possible only by an evolution of German policies, which will be explained later. Here is also a Gaullist influence or, from the American point of view, an accommodation of the prevailing mood in Europe. According to the Gaullist theory, East European countries follow Russian leadership because they are afraid of German revanchism, rather than by duress of Russian armed forces, a theory to be exposed to a premature test in the Czechoslovakian suppression two years later.

The regular ministerial meeting of the North Atlantic Council held in Paris, December 15-16, 1966, adopted a communique, which was rather unique in its history, obviously reflecting the changing mood of its member nations in that year.

First it declared, "The Alliance has demonstrated its value by successfully averting threats to peace and safeguarding the security of the Atlantic area. By its defensive strength, including its effective means of deterrence as well as by maintaining its solidarity, the Alliance has produced the basis for the present marked *reduction of tension* in Europe." This is the basic theory and justification of the alliance in its context with detente. Then it referred to Germany and said, "So long as Germany continues to be divided there cannot be a genuine and stable settlement in Europe. The peaceful progress of Europe must proceed from reciprocal confidence and trust, which will take time to grow from sustained policies of cooperative effort and better understanding on both sides. It means especially removing barriers to freer and more friendly reciprocal exchanges between countries of different social and economic systems." And it elaborated further its policies to secure better relations with the Soviet Union and the states of Eastern Europe in the political, economic, social, scientific, and cultural fields. Couve de Murville, the French foreign minister who was described as a Hi-Fi Gaullist, was reported to have commented on that meeting "Now East-West detente is in fashion, but only a few years ago this kind of idea was considered as criminal." We should not forget, however, that the attitude of NATO was again stiffened after the Czechoslovakian invasion, at least in its rhetoric.

Evolution of German Attitude

Behind all these spectacular changes in the attitude of the Western alliance there was always an evolution of the German attitude. It is no exaggeration to say the tempo of the entire process of East-West detente in the 1960s and early 1970s has been set by the pace of gradual changes in the German attitude. The German problem is the heart of the European problem and not to be dealt with lightly. Moreover, West Germany is a very important member of the NATO alliance and the feelings of the German people and the impact of the alliance on the domestic politics of Germany should be always respected. Even General De Gaulle, while advocating East-West detente from the end of the 1950s and often showing a different opinion from other NATO countries, rarely contradicted the fundamental positions of West Germany. As far as I remember, the only case in which he differed in expression from the West German official stand was that he insisted on the maintenance of the status quo of German territorial borders, both East and West. Beyond this point he carefully avoided discussing the future of East Germany, while always pointing out that the German question was the core of the European question. The importance of the "Peace Notes" of West Germany should be considered in that framework. On March 25, 1966 West

Germany sent identical notes to all countries with which it had diplomatic relations, as well as to the countries of Eastern Europe and to the Arab states. The note said, while stressing the unification of Germany as the primary objective of the German people, "The Government of the Federal Republic of Germany has repeatedly stated that the German people would be prepared to make sacrifices for the sake of their reunification. They are determined to solve this problem by peaceful means only." Rejecting the notion of "German revanchism," the note said "The thought of another war, which would destroy whole countries and nations, even continents, is unbearable to them (German people). They want to help insure that such a catastrophe can never happen, and in this wish they know that they are at one with all reasonable people." It proposed, above all, that (1) all non-nuclear states belonging to military alliances in the East or the West should renounce the production of nuclear weapons and submit to international control, and (2) the Federal Republic was ready to exchange formal declarations with the Soviet Union, Poland, Czechoslovakia, and any other East European state whereby each side would give an agreement to the other not to use force in the settlement of international disputes.

It is obvious that President Johnson's speech and the NATO communique discussed above could take place only after this declaration of West Germany. After this the so-called detente policy of the middle 1960s surged into the European scene as if a dam had been broken. As we will see later, this was only the beginning of the long, zig-zag course which has taken place in the past decade, and is a result of the long process of evolution since the beginning of the 1960s. If the year 1966 was marked by the official confirmation of a detente policy by the Western nations, the years 1962 and 1963 may be characterized as the period which prepared for this change.

The policy of peaceful coexistence of Khrushchev was confirmed in the Cuban crisis of 1962. As a result it ruled out the possibility of a total nuclear war and the possibility of a full-scale military engagement between the United States and the USSR on the European front, which is the most likely place for a nuclear war to start. And in the Berlin Wall crisis preceding it, the Western allies did not act as firmly as some Germans expected, and eventually allowed the stabilization of East Germany, which was on the verge of collapse.[b] These facts practically ruled out the possibility of the use of force as a method to achieve German unification. The partial test ban treaty must have had an equally significant influence on West Germany. Although West Germany had committed itself vis-à-vis Western nations not to arm with nuclear weapons, the possibility of German nuclear armament had always been a potential pressure on the Eastern bloc in connection with the future development of the German problem. The partial test ban treaty in effect deprived Germany of the possibility of conducting a nuclear test by the decision of the three powers, apparently

[b]See Jean Edward Smith, *The Defense of Berlin* (Baltimore, Md., Johns Hopkins Press, 1963).

without the approval of West Germany. Thus the maintenance of the status quo in Europe was presented to West Germany as an irrevocable reality. In fact, about the same time the nuclear test ban treaty was concluded, West Germany started to adopt a more "flexible" diplomacy and proceeded to conclude trade agreements and to exchange trade representatives with East European countries, such as Poland, Hungary, and Rumania.

It always takes time, however, for a professed official policy to reflect the political reality, particularly when the problem is as difficult as the German question. Detente policy based on recognition of the status quo is contrary to the principle, adopted since the Adenauer period, that every step toward detente should be combined with the progress of German unification, and any step for detente without substantial progress toward such unification should be rejected. Therefore, we can term the ten years between 1963 and 1973 as a period in which this principle was modified gradually. And the Peace Notes of 1966 constituted a watershed in the sense that this modification was officially announced.

The Rise and Fall, and Then Rebirth
of Detente Policy

As we have seen, there was certainly something unusual in the mood of detente in the middle of the 1960s. Some experts pointed out, perhaps accurately, that it was too late and too much. It was too late when the Western nations, which had even tabooed the word "peaceful coexistence" in their official statements during the period of Khrushchev's repeated approaches, suddenly moved toward a detente policy vis-à-vis the Brezhnev regime after the fall of Khrushchev. It was too much that they approached East European nations with fanfare when the Russians had already started showing wariness against the adverse effect of too close a relation with Western nations and relaxation of the Eastern solidarity.

In fact, looking back now on the history of that period, the German and West European effort for detente in 1966 was facing a really formidable resistance from the Russian side from its very beginning. The Russian reply to the Peace Note was entirely acrimonious, saying that the Oder-Neisse frontier was "final and unalterable," that it was "not by courtesy of the German Federal Republic that the European States and their Frontiers exist," and that the whole policy of the German Federal government was "subordinated to one purpose—to obtain the status of a nuclear power and try . . . to restore the German Reich with all its pretensions."

The Kiesinger government which was formed late in 1966 absorbed new energy from the SPD in implementing its Ostpolitik hitherto formulated by the CDU and CSU. The main objective of the Ostpolitik of the Kiesinger government was normalization of relations with the Eastern European countries. It modified the interpretation of the so-called Hallstein doctrine, which had prevented West Germany from having diplomatic relations with any country which had diplomatic relations with East Germany at the same time, so that it recognized exceptions to the Hallstein doctrine for the cases which were the result of the inevitable circumstances of the postwar period, implying that certain East European countries' choice of an East German partner was forced upon them.

West Germany had success in establishing diplomatic relations with Rumania in January 1967 and in exchanging trade representatives with Czechoslovakia in the summer. However, its negotiation for diplomatic relations with Czechoslovakia, Hungary, and Poland faced various difficulties. Soviet displeasure was quite obvious. On the occasion of German-Rumanian normalization the Soviet Union issued a statement upholding the solidarity of the Eastern bloc and criticizing West Germany for neo-Nazism and militarism. In March a new treaty of mutual cooperation, which was then called the "iron triangle," was concluded among East Germany, Poland, and Czechoslovakia. Also similar treaties were concluded between Bulgaria and Poland in April and Bulgaria and East Germany in September. Thus the West German efforts were frustrated and it had to give up for the time being its goal of diplomatic normalization with Poland and Czechoslovakia, which were considered to be the principal objectives. Instead it had to be satisfied with normalization with Yugoslavia, to which, strictly speaking, the application of the exception to the Hallstein doctrine was considered rather doubtful at the beginning. It became increasingly clear at that time that the Soviet Union was determined to control the entire gamut of relations of East European countries with West Germany.[c] Being aware of this fact, West Germany was already reorganizing its efforts toward more direct dealings with the Soviet Union, but any real progress in this approach had to wait for a later period, in which the immediate effect of the Czechoslovakian incident had dissipated and the mood and necessity for detente slowly returned.

The negotiations for non-use of force, which constitutes one of the main objectives of Ostpolitik under the Peace Note, also encountered snags. Negotiations had been conducted between the Soviet Union and West Germany from 1966 to 1968, and many documents were exchanged covering a wide range of subjects including the Oder-Neisse border, the Munich Agreement, Berlin's status, and so on. However, in July 1968, a month before the Czechoslovakian invasion, the Soviets sent the harshest note ever to Germany and suddenly published all documents of the negotiations of the preceding two years in *Izvestia*, and thus the negotiations were suspended. The reason the Soviets suspended the negotiations was not clear, but the relation to the coming Czechoslovakian invasion was quite obvious. The Soviet Union must have felt the situation in East Europe in the spring of 1968 was extremely serious, and

---

[c]The USSR's effort to synchronize these relations is at present being confirmed by the Crimea meetings of the Eastern European leaders and by the conduct of the European Security Conference (CSCE).

thought it inappropriate to continue the negotiation for the non-use of force with West Germany, which must have the effect of easing the East Europeans fear toward German revanchism, or the effect of losing the pretext of German revanchism, if it was already largely a fiction.

In any event, the Czechoslovakian invasion dealt a tremendous blow to the mood of optimism for detente and morally discouraged a further approach to the Soviet Union, and Ostpolitik was checked for a while.

However, the Ostpolitik of West Germany and the entire detente policy of the Western nations is a policy without any alternative since maintenance of the status quo is a fact of life under strict application of East-West peaceful coexistence. Likewise for the Soviet Union, it is desirable to stabilize the status quo in Europe and to increase economic exchanges with the West. Therefore, as the "normalization" of Czechoslovakia progresses and the Soviet Union regains its confidence by having the East European situation under control, things were bound to return to the status prior to 1968. The Russian side proposed the reopening of negotiations for the non-use of force and West Germany responded reluctantly, at least at the beginning, but then they reached an agreement in 1970. Since then the renewed Ostpolitik led to the Soviet-German and Polish-German Treaties (May 1972), a four-power agreement on Berlin (June 1972), a provisional signature on the treaty with East Germany (November 1972), and other final touches of its Ostpolitik following the victory of the Brandt government in the general elections (November 1972). A full interpretation of the years 1972-1973 in comparision with 1966 and 1963 may be premature, however, and should be left to future study. Nevertheless, one characteristic is that both sides are interested in detente. I notice also more realism and that neither side is without economic difficulties within their economic systems.

What Has Detente Policy Achieved?

It is not hard to imagine that the promotion of Ostpolitik required many difficult decisions for West Germany. German territory was reduced by the Versailles Treaty to an area less than that actually inhabited by German nationals. Then as a result of the Second World War Germany was not only divided but also lost part of its territory to the occupation by Russia and Poland without German consent. Declaration of the non-use of force and all the other agreements between West Germany and East European countries imply one thing: recognition of the status quo.

One can imagine what drastic decisions West Germany had to make only by imagining a similar situation in Asia. It is as if the People's Republic of China were to declare the non-use of force with the United States and call for solution of the Taiwan problem only by peaceful means and then to conclude a treaty with Taiwan and have Chinese embassies in foreign capitals side by side with those of Taiwan. Some might say President Nixon's initiative with Peking has achieved the same result in a more subtle and practical way. It is clear, however, that the form is still vastly different and we have yet to see how the new relations work out.

If we compare the Russian and German positions before 1966, it is clear that the German side made unilateral concessions, at least in form. With all these concessions what was gained by West Germany? All the comments in favor of the achievements of Ostpolitik say that it contributed to the promotion of detente in Europe. Some comments do not even say it achieved a detente but that it only opened the gate to detente. It is not quite clear whether the gain is the detente itself or what detente may produce in the future.

Here is the difficulty in explaining or defining a detente policy. It is hard to find an official explanation for it from the documents of Western governments. Moreover, the reaction of the Soviet Union against Western measures entitled "detente policy" are often quite indirect and vague. If we rely only on the hard facts or unequivocal quotations, we have even to cast doubt on the accuracy of my previous observation that the Eastern side reacted against the Western detente policy in the period between 1966 to 1968. The most we can say is that the measures taken by the Eastern nations in that period give the impression that they reacted against the Western detente policy.

Some reasons for the vagueness of the Western explanation derive from the fact that the objectives of detente policy differ according to the individuals who advocate it, and that the greater the objective is, the longer the time required, and nobody is certain about its real effects. Furthermore, the vagueness may sometimes be intentional, the real objective being unmentionable in diplomatic language.

It is a fact that the detente policy began with the maintenance of the status quo on the European front under U.S.-USSR peaceful coexistence. But no Western nations explain the detente policy as merely maintaining the status quo, even though this may be the only substance for the time being. Of course, recognition of the status quo itself has some significance. For some individuals who genuinely fear a resurgent Germany, the maintenance of the division itself may be significant. And some German individuals who aspire to "independent diplomacy" may welcome the situation in which Germany is freed from various international and internal commitments made during the period of the cold war, and able to behave freely as a nation as it is in the existing status quo. Official explanations of Western governments, however, take the posture that the detente policy seeks something beyond the maintenance of the status quo. In diplomatic language, they propose a detente policy under which they first expand economic contracts, and then various exchanges, build up a relation of mutual understanding, and finally resolve pending problems through the mutual understanding thus attained. If we look into the matter a little more deeply many contradictions appear. The pending problems of Europe must certainly include the existing division of Europe. If this is so, detente policy is seeking a change of the status quo by recognizing the status quo.

President Johnson, in 1966, stated "That division must be healed peacefully. It must be healed with the consent of East European countries and the Soviet Union." This approach should be welcome by the East. They are talking, however, about the question of Germany. In that speech the United States is supporting the unification of Germany, and the East is categorically opposed to it. The purpose of the West is unification, and improvement of the environment is the method. It means that they expect a change of attitude in East European countries as the environment changes. What kind of environmental change will induce such a change of attitude of the East? The best and perfect result will be gained if pluralism emerges and ideological confrontation eventually ceases to exist. At least their attitude on the ideological confrontation should be softened, combined with more emphasis on the idea of a new international balance of power to be achieved.

Here I might propose a simplified model as follows. Family A asserts that its daughter shall never marry the son of the neighboring Family B. Family B privately hopes to get the daughter of A as a bride for its son and as its method proposes a good neighbor relation between the two families and tries to enlarge contacts between them.

The objective of Family B is never found in the words and Behavior of B, but Family A is afraid that, as the contacts increase, the daughter and people around her might start entertaining favorable feelings toward the son of Family B. Since it is hard to refuse a good neighborly relation, both for moral and financial reasons, Family A maintains an ambivalent attitude. In case the daughter becomes overwhelmed by emotion, Family A has to lock her up and cut all contacts with Family B temporarily. As a result the relations between the two families cool down, but Family B has no other alternative than to renew the effort to gain the favor of Family A, and Family A has no reason to refuse the relation. So the good neighborly relation is resumed again in an atmosphere of ambivalence.

This model appears to fit some aspects of East-West relations in Europe over the past few years. But here again I must make the reservation that no official document or hard fact can underwrite this theoretical model. It is by nature impossible to quote a diplomatic document on such a delicate matter. It was with surprising frankness the Chinese declared that peaceful coexistence is no more than a tactic, but this kind of frankness is rarely found in diplomacy. And the Chinese could even now be embarrassed badly by this former frankness.

Some Theories for Detente Policy

In view of the difficulties in finding official documents which explain the true intentions of detente policy, I should like to quote from two sources which I believe give clues to some motives behind the detente policy.

One such source is the *Memoirs* of General de Gaulle. As we have seen, some motives of detente policy are unmentionable in diplomatic language, but in the case of De Gaulle we can learn his ideas from his memoirs, which were mostly written when he was out of power and before being nominated to the presidency of the French Republic. Because of the surprising consistency of his thought during his career, we may quite safely surmise what he had in mind while he was pursuing a detente policy after assuming office.

Another such source is the so-called convergence theory. This theory has an established position among the theories of comparative study of the economic systems of the Communist and capitalist worlds. I should like to try to introduce some of them and to discuss their political implications.

The Gaullist Concept of East-West Relations

De Gaulle's greatest preoccupation in foreign policy was, of course, Germany, with which France fought major wars three times in less than 100 years. In his plan for the postwar world De Gaulle states in his memoirs that the primary target is elimination of the threat from Germany. According to him, Russia certainly controls East Europe in its totalitarian method, but if Germany ceases to be a threat, control over its satellites must become unjustifiable oppression and is bound to face rebellion sooner or later. If the Kremlin wants to maintain oppression, it must go against national sentiment in these countries—no regime can continue to ignore national sentiment.

The way to eliminate the German threat, as suggested by De Gaulle at that time, was to decentralize the German administrative system. This particular idea itself was not realized, but the general idea is still valid according to this. When West German good neighborly diplomacy is successful and East European nations no longer recognize the existence of a German threat, the Soviet Union will lose one of the strongest justifications for the solidarity of the Eastern bloc and eventually will have to yield to East European nationalism. Even if this intention exists behind German Ostpolitik, there is no way that it may be told to the outside in diplomatic language or expressed in words of responsible statesmen.

De Gaulle's plan anticipates not only catching the East European states off guard, but, also, changes in their political and social systems within themselves. He says:

The Eastern Bloc is under a certain special philosophy and principle, in other words autocracy, and refusing our participation or mutual understanding. The Bloc has an ambition to conquer the world and does not want liberty, equality and fraternity. France and its allies should maintain the power to contain this bloc for a certain period of time. This period means until detente is achieved first by the evolution of the internal situation of the Bloc and by the inevitable expression of humanity, and then, perhaps, cooperation between free peoples is achieved and the peace is built upon it.

In other remarks De Gaulle elaborates on the evolution in the international scene and on the Western policy based on it as maintaining "the existing peace, in the hope that we can achieve detente first in the future and the final goal of entente, thus bringing peaceful and secured life to mankind."

He also says:

We have to defend ourselves as long as the East does not give up its ambition. This does not deprive us of hope. The hope consists of expectation of future changes in Eastern states. Evolution will show its results in the countries which have been and still are always deeply humanistic and nationalistic; they are Poland, Czechoslovakia, Hungary, Rumania, Bulgaria, Albania, and the USSR. Time may come when these countries prefer human rights, that is liberty, equality and fraternity—to bondage. This day will bring about peace and prosperity of the world.

In examining this statement, the intention of General De Gaulle is crystal clear. He understands that communism is an "outdated ideology" and will disappear in time. As a policy to be adopted by the West he proposes to maintain deterrent capability until the time when Communist ideology perishes and a true mutual understanding is born between the two blocs.

It is natural that the Soviets, while welcoming General De Gaulle's ostensibly secessionist tendency from the Western alliance, became increasingly wary of De Gaulle's intention. De Gaulle's detente policy, which was unfolded in East Europe during his tenure in office, was received in these countries with enthusiasm and emotion, combined with deep suspicion, and achieved little concrete results. Of course De Gaulle himself was the most pessimistic of all advocates of a detente policy. He did not even claim to have achieved a detente, but said that he had tried to achieve it. He must have known that things would not move fast.

De Gaulle's detente policy is based on macroscopic historical vision, according to which the only important elements in international politics are the relations of power among states and nations, and national and humanistic aspirations. His philosophy certainly has a truth of its own. It is, however, often inappropriate in a short-term or middle-term analysis, because of its underestimation of the ideological side in the present circumstance, where communism is still a political power which represents half the world, even fifty years after the death of Lenin. On the contrary, the convergence theory, to be explained next, squarely faces the fact of life that the Communist world does exist and still possesses vitality to survive for some time, and seeks the possibility of detente between two systems.

Convergence Theory

Convergence theories in the Western world are essentially economic theories. Each theory takes a different form with different emphasis, but all believe that there must be a common pattern in the economic development of human societies and that there must be an optimum form of economic society which maximizes the economic goal which the human race seeks, whether it is a society of welfare or a society with the maximum aggregate productive power. It also believes that human society should be and is progressing toward this one optimum condition, and therefore the ultimate goal of both Communist and capitalist worlds is inevitably common. They do not discuss the political effect of convergence very often, but its political implication is obvious. If the difference in the economic systems disappears, then presumably confrontation between the two systems themselves and therefore East-West confrontation, is bound to disappear. Of course, as we will discuss later, the reality is not as simple as this, but its optimism for the future of mankind undeniably influenced the thinking of responsible people in the 1960s.

At first, the convergence theory was primarily academic, but as the Soviet Union and other East European countries started introducing so-called economic reforms in the middle of the 60s, the possibility of convergence was taken up in the mass media. For example, the *New York Times*, commenting on Premier Kosygin's speech on economic reform in the Party Central Committee in September 1965, said that the new Soviet economic reform looked like capitalism. Then Soviet reactions against it began appearing in Russian newspapers with the time lag of a few years.

Western Theories of Convergence. First let me present a few convergence theories which I think are typical of Western thinking and which have had significant influence on East-West relations.

W.W. Rostow's thought was expressed in *Stages of Economic Growth*, published in 1960, one year before J. Tinbergen published his essay *Do Communist and Free Economies Show a Converging Pattern?*

The advent of these theories was perhaps not without relation to the condition of the Soviet economy. In spite of the tremendous damage of the Second World War, in which the USSR is believed to have lost twenty million of its people, the Soviet Union succeeded, until the middle of the 1950s, in maintaining a high economic growth rate with its policy of extreme concentration on heavy industry, except for the short *Malenkov* period. This economic growth was demonstrated in a dramatic way by the development of the ICBM and the Sputnik well ahead of the United States. The theme of superiority of the socialist economic system was played repeatedly and produced a sense of crisis in the Western world.

In retrospect, however, the Soviet Union's high growth policy based on heavy industry was approaching a certain limit toward the latter half of the 1950s. The new five-year plan which was started in 1956 obviously did not work well and was suspended in 1958, and a new seven-year plan was started in 1959. At the time when Khrushchev proposed to overtake the American economy, various problems of Soviet economy were already surfacing. In the first half of the 1960s, a slowdown in the growth of the Soviet economy became a real problem and in the agricultural field there was an actual decline in 1963.

Convergence theories reflect this reality of the Soviet economy and the reactions of Western society to it. For the first time Western society had to recognize that the Soviet economy had a strength competitive with Western economy and furthermore had to face, though rather dubiously, the Soviet pretension that its economic system was superior to that of the West and would overtake it in the future. While they had to concede Soviet economic and technological success up to the middle of the 1950s, they were not certain about its future. Nor at the end of the 1950s were they quite certain about the future of the Western economy, not foreseeing the golden 60s of the Western economy. Therefore their theory is marked by efforts to find out the actual status and prospect of the Soviet economy and by both defensive pride in the Western economy and cautiousness about its future.

Rostow thought it possible to identify all societies, in their economic dimensions, as lying within one of five categories: the traditional society, the precondition for take-off, the take-off, the drive to maturity, and the age of high mass-consumption. According to him the United States entered the age of high mass-consumption in the early 1920s while the Soviet Union was still in the drive to maturity in the latter half of the 1950s. He says that at the moment the Soviet Union is a society technically ready for the age of high mass-consumption, but, in terms of the stages of growth, the USSR is a nation seeking to convert its maturity into world primacy by postponing or damping the advent of the age of high mass-consumption.

Rostow's theory may belong to the convergence theory school in the sense that it explains economic development of all societies under one criterion, i.e., productivity, regardless of their ideology, and conceives this process of development as the inevitable course for any nation. His theory is less diplomatic than other convergence theories, which suggest mutual rapprochement of the two systems. He says that communism is likely to wither in the age of high mass-consumption and this, almost certainly, is well understood in Moscow. His argument is full of pride in the American economy, as the latter policymaker of that country, and an ideologically militant analyst honestly reflecting the spirit of his age—the age of the cold war and the "American Century." Some may call his theory more a "submergence theory" of Communist economy than a convergence theory, but we have to recognize that some of his forecasts proved to be accurate in contrasting the situation of the Western and Communist economies in the 1960s. Moreover, his theory in some respects is still valid now that the high mood for convergence in the later 1960s has subsided and the ideological confrontation still remains.

J. Tinbergen also made a close scholarly analysis of both the Communist and the capitalist economic systems. First he enumerated major changes which have occurred in the Communist system since the Russian Revolution, such as the introduction of specialized management instead of workers' autonomous operation, wages reflecting productivity instead of absolute equality, utilization of money and interest, consumer choice, and so on. Then he described the changes the free world has undergone, such as the growth of the public sector, importance of taxes as regulators of economic activity, limitation to free competition for technical reasons and increasing governmental power and intervention in various fields of national life and economy, although he stresses the great differences which exist between the two systems. I have no intention of summarizing his entire theory here, but will only outline its main thrust. He points out problems which have to be solved in respective societies and considers that the efforts for their solution might bring about further tendencies toward a converging movement. And he thinks that this is true particularly in regard to the main question about the degree of decentralization in production decisions and planning, and that it is to some extent also true in the process of price formation. Finally, he believes that if we consult welfare economics, in principle, it tells us about the conditions which the optimum pattern of organization of society has to fulfill, and that the optimum pattern is not necessarily the free enterprise system. Like other convergence theorists Tinbergen considers that the possibility of total war stems partly from difference of opinion between the East and West as to the best form of social economic system. Although he is very cautious about the actual possibility of convergence, one might say his theory is still based on optimism that mankind may have a chance for a stable peace through convergence of the two systems.

The New Industrial State by J.K. Galbraith was first published in 1967. While the theories of Rostow and Tinbergen were published at a time when peaceful coexistence was not yet stable and the Russian economy faced a turning point, the period in which Galbraith's book was introduced was marked by a growing sense of relaxation of tension between East and West and also by Soviet adoption of a new economic policy which enabled it to regain a tempo of economic progress. In Galbraith's book we can see more optimism for the future of convergence of the two systems. Here again we can note the mood of the latter half of the 1960s.

In order to explain his thought I will simply borrow his phrases, which are too well composed to be paraphrased. The principal theme is the stress of the "industrial system," which means "the world of the few hundred technically dynamic, massively capitalized and highly organized corporations."[d] According

---

[d]John Kenneth Galbraith, *The New Industrial State* (Boston: Houghton Mifflin Company, 1972), p. 9.

to Galbraith, "General Motors, General Electric and U.S. Steel are an ultimate achievement,"[e] with the "technostructure" which has developed in them. He believes, "Such reflections (that the industrial system is not transitory but something on which attention should be fixed in considering the future) on the future would also emphasize the convergent tendencies of industrial societies, however different their popular or ideological billing."[f] After giving reasons for a Soviet-type producing system to work in a very similar way, he says:

Thus convergence between the two ostensibly different industrial systems occurs at all fundamental points. This is an exceedingly fortunate thing. In time, and perhaps in less time than may be imagined, it will dispose of the notion of inevitable conflict based on irreconcilable difference. . . . To recognize that industrial systems are convergent in their development will, one imagines, help toward agreement on the common dangers in weapons competition, on ending it or shifting it to more benign areas . . .

Preparing against the argument of overestimation of the influence of the industrial system on the question of the entire sytem, he continues:

Given the deep dependence of the industrial system on the state and the nature of its motivational relationship to the state, i.e., its identification with public goals and the adaptation of these to its needs, the industrial system will not long be regarded as something apart from government. Rather it will increasingly be seen as part of a much larger complex which embraces both the industrial system and the state.[g]

Galbraith also stresses the relation of the industrial system to the cold war. He says:

In its more simplistic outline, the relation of the Cold War to the needs of the industrial system has been remarkably close. It is a relentless, implacable, permanent, but ultimately benign, struggle with the world Communist movement as led by the Soviet Union. It is occasioned by the differences in economic systems from which, primarily, are derived differences in individual liberty . . . The highly organized and planned system of the Soviets requires the subordination of the individual to the goals of the state. . . . No such constraint by organization or planning is required by the Western system of free enterprise. . . . The incompatibility of the systems and the associated evangelism lead directly to military competition.[h]

When one applies Galbraith's theory of convergence to this notion of the origin of the cold war, one soon reaches an optimistic conclusion for the future of world peace and prosperity.

---

[e]Ibid., p. 391.
[f]Ibid., p. 392.
[g]Ibid., p. 394-95.
[h]Ibid., p. 330-31.

As to be examined later, this is the most important and intriguing problem of the convergence theory: its relations with the political and sociological evolution of the Communist society. In economic terms it may be possible and practical to find similarities in both systems and a necessity for the further tendency for convergence. The question is how to relate examples of similarity to the overall relation of the two systems. In an unsophisticated example we remember that at the early stage of the East-West thaw, Western travelers were impressed by the fact that they found human beings similar to themselves behind the iron curtain and that Russian coal was not red but as black as coal in the capitalist world. This kind of mood induced some people to accept the naive fallacy that no iron curtain existed. The relation between a political system and an economic system is a very complicated matter. In fact there may be more examples in international politics denying any significant relation between economic and political systems than supporting the original Marxist idea of the relation between an economic lower structure and a political upper structure. Some phenomena even make us doubt if the Soviet system is an economic system under Marxism rather than a political system from the very beginning.

Before moving to the next section, let us touch upon the policy implication of the convergence theory. The convergence theory is one of economic dynamics. It expects changes and hopes the change will take place expeditiously. It hopes that as the Communist economy develops faster Communist countries will be stimulated to adjust themselves politically to the accelerated growth, and "liberalization" will be the result. An apparently paradoxical theorem of detente policy, such as "to improve economic conditions of the East contributes to the Western security" is based on this kind of thinking. Of course, economic exchanges are always beneficial to both sides, and even the most conservative people are not opposed as long as it would not harm Western defense materially and morally.

A similar thing may be said about the Gaullist concept of detente, which expects the inevitable expression of humanistic and nationalistic feeling in the people of the East. Here also various personnel and cultural exchanges and contacts will certainly improve the chance of the evolution expected.

In fact, in the current international politics between East and West, it is quite often seen that what the West is seeking is to enlarge the scope and quantity of various exchanges and intercourses, while what the East is seeking is state-to-state political concessions.

Russian Reaction to the Convergence Theory. Soviet reactions against the convergence theory became conspicuous in 1968. Going through representative Russian economic magazines such as the *Problems of Economics, World Economics and International Relations*, and the *Planned Economy*, prior to 1968 we find only one article on convergence: "New versions of the Theory of the "Transformation" of Capitalism by Bregel, in the *Problems of Economics*,

August 1967. In January, 1968, *World Economics and International Relations* carried two articles on the convergence theory, one written by Bregel, which I will introduce below. In February, the *Problems of Economics* carried "Convergence Theory and its Reality" by Cherbakov. And the word "convergence" began to appear and be discussed extensively in Soviet mass media, including of course *Pravda* and *Izvestia*, through 1968, 1969, and to the present.[i]

This sudden increase in comments on the convergence theory may be due to the publication of Galbraith's *The New Industrial State* in 1967, since one of the two articles which appeared in January 1968 was a book review of it. There may be a more fundamental reason however. Exactly as pointed out in *Pravda* on September 1, 1969, they considered the convergence theory equivalent to the notorious "bridge-building" proposed by President Johnson in 1966 and the "Ostpolitik" of revanchists in Bonn. It was a reaction against the detente policy of the West since 1966, as well as a reaction against the convergence theory itself. Since 1966 a mood of detente pervaded the East European countries and a serious situation was already engendered in Czechoslovakia in December 1967 and January 1968. Furthermore, the severe criticism of West German "revanchism" seemed to indicate a fear of German social democracy as both a theoretical and practical form of convergence which could be particularly seductive for Eastern Europeans. Russian ideologues must have felt that something had to be done.

Reaction was initiated by a well thought out economic theory. Bregel's "Convergence Theory of the Two Economic Systems" in January 1968 may still be the most comprehensive comment on the convergence theory from the Russian side.

First Bregel summarized the Western theory of convergence as follows: (1) Similarities between the two economic systems are said to be growing. The emphasis is not on the similarity itself but on the growing trend, for if a fundamental difference remains in spite of some similarities, there will be no question of convergence. Therefore, in the convergence theory, accumulation of common characteristics, rather than the static resemblance, is emphasized. (2) The difference is supposed to disappear gradually as the result of rapprochement. Bourgeois thinkers used to insist on the possibility of capitalistic evolution in the Soviet economy, but this is not a convergence theory. Convergence is supposed to be mutual between the capitalist economy and Socialist economy. (3) The theory predicts an ultimate evolution into a "mixed" type of socioeconomic system combining characteristics and elements of both capitalism and socialism. This summary itself is a fair one, particularly in that it conceives of the convergence theory as dynamic rather than static, but in his comments Bregel tends to point out mainly static differences and comments very little on the possibility of future evolution.

---

[i]For an excellent recent survey see Leon Gouré et al., *Convergence of Communism and Capitalism: The Soviet View*, Miami, Center for Advanced International Studies, University of Miami, 1973.

Bregel also introduces some convergence theories and says "the most thorough and earnest propagandist of the convergence theory is Tinbergen and further refers to Galbraith, but not to Rostow. The fact that Rostow foresaw a unilateral change in the Communist system may have made Bregel exclude him from the list according to his definitions in the above paragraph.

Bregel criticizes the convergence theory as follows: First he says that there is a fundamental methodological mistake in applying a technical approach to an economic system, which should be ideologically defined. He insists on separating technology or partial productive processes from the entire economic system; similarities in the former he says, are irrelevant to the latter. Here Bregel refuses to consider the eventual influence of evolution in technology and of productive processes on ideology. We might describe his comment as tantamount to saying that the process of launching a satellite may be similar in the United States and the USSR, but the entire economic systems behind them are completely different—a simple static argument.

Secondly, Bregel makes a very ideological argument that a capitalist state which serves the interest of monopoly is fundamentally different from the Socialist states which serve the interest of the people, however much the role of the state may grow in a capitalist economy. Here he engages in a limited discussion about the dynamic relation between a state and a productive organization, such as an industrial system.

Thirdly, Bregel refuses a concept of decentralization of state authorities to industries, arguing that all Soviet productive enterprises are national and not private and therefore the effect of economic reforms is a mere shift of function within a nationalized productive organization and does not mean the weakening of state authority. Here he merely points out the static form of ownership and does not confront the nature and prospect of decentralization.

I have to set aside other economic arguments of Bregel's since they are not germane here. His theory is, in sum, that the capitalist system is fundamentally different from the Socialist system, and it is wrong to pursue only the quantitative differences of economic planning of two systems, neglecting the differences which exist in basic principles.

Bregel also discusses a political side of the convergence theory, quoting Tinbergen's observation that the difference of views on the socioeconomic system between the West and East is an important element in the possibility of a total war. Bregel says that it is a positive moment in the argument of supporters of the convergence theory that they recognize the principle of peaceful coexistence, but it is impossible to accept their fundamental attitude to relate peaceful coexistence with the "notorious" convergence theory. He points out, correctly, that the question of peaceful coexistence emerged as a fact of history and became a practical question of the coexistence of two different, and even confronting social systems, and the necessity and practicability of such coexistence for the survival of mankind has been proved in theory and in practice. He then criticizes the interpretation of peaceful coexistence by Tinbergen and others, saying that irrespective of their personal stands on peaceful coexistence, it gives the advocates of the cold war and anticommunism a motive to declare that it is useless to consider peaceful coexistence as long as there is no convergence of the two systems. He declares that a Marxist-Leninist approach to the question of coexistence is to recognize the fact of confrontation between socialism and capitalism, to conceive of the coexistence of states of different social systems as one form of class struggle, and to recognize the possibility and necessity of the maintenance of peaceful relations between Socialist states and capitalist states. Very clearly he stresses the difference in the two systems as the base for peaceful coexistence, and definitely not the possibility of convergence. This stand was reconfirmed and emphasized at the Twenty-Third Party Congress and in many official comments in that period.

Bregel concludes that the convergence theory is the newest and the most intricate form of bourgeois ideology. Since capitalists must give up the idea that capitalism is infallible, they seek the salvation of capitalism by recognizing some points in the Socialist system, and at the same time, gamble on the capitalistic evolution of the Socialist system; they hope to make incompatibles compatible and describe the historical evolution of a society in a reverse fashion; mankind is not moving toward a mongrel capitalism—socialism, but is moving toward a Communist society.

In the late 1960s we could quote dozens of Soviet criticisms of convergence theory, made by party leaders, ideologues, and academics appearing in various publications. Their rhetoric is sometimes more acrimonious, but theoretically the above comments of Bregel cover the ground. The Communist leaders strongly assert their ideological puritanism,

There is not and cannot be any non-class or above-class ideology in a world rent by class warfare. . . . There is no room for neutrality of compromises in the ideological struggle. Marxist-Lenninists reject the opportunist thesis about a peaceful coexistence of ideologies. . . . This demands a consistent class line in education, correct and clear ideological attitudes, the further strengthening of revolutionary vigilance, and a constant struggle against apoliticalism, the survival of private ownership, Philistine moods, manifestations of nihilistic attitudes toward socialist achievements, and the appearance of bourgeois and revisionist views,[j]

and warn repeatedly against those who would build bridges,

the advocates of the "theory of bridges" do not conceal their intention to use this theory in order to infiltrate bourgeois ideas and culture and to subvert the socialist system.[k]

---

[j]"Theses" of the CPSU, reported in *Pravda*, December 23, 1969.

[k]D. Shevliagin, *Pravda*, June 14, 1967.

Building bridges is seen as a ploy to divide the "socialist commonwealth;" convergence theory as a ploy to confuse the real issues; and "de-ideologization" as a form of ideological disarmament.

The World of Sakharov. Before leaving the subject of the convergence theory, I should like to make a brief study of particular cases in connection with it; Sakharov's vision of convergence and the Chinese cultural revolution.

No Western theorist on convergence is certain about the world after convergence. The convergence theory, as skillfully summarized by Bregel, consists of stages: increase of similarities, mutual approach, and evolution into a single socioeconomic system. It is not clear, however, in what time frame this would take place and what the entire shape of the world would be after convergence. This demonstrates the limitation of the discipline of Western economic theorists. As they try to relate the vision of the best economic system to the question of peace and war, what they try to infer is quite obvious; but they politely refrain from infringing on the territorial right of political scientists whose discipline, in turn, prevents them from taking an optimistic stand. They sometimes refer vaguely to the possibility or hope for detente as ideology lapses, but most experts on communism are wary of even referring to such a possibility. There is no schematic way of relating political phenomena with economic ones. Economic liberalization would not directly affect the administrative structure for internal affairs; it may, at least in a short term, have an adverse effect on tightening of control. Furthermore, even if one admits the possibility of changes in the political system, the question of peace and war could be a completely different matter. War existed even before the Russian Revolution. It is hardly absurd to look for examples of wars fought between states of the same system—all wars in history before the Second World War fall in this category. On the question of peace and war the only practical way of thinking may be to combine conventional power politics, based on history, tradition and national aspiration, with the possibility of lapses in ideology as suggested by De Gaulle or Brzezinski.

Sakharov's world of convergence is unique in this sense. In addition to his amateur position in politics, we can see traditional Russian temerity and genius in his vision. Moreover, he himself has admitted imperfections in his argument and invited comments.

Sakharov describes his concept of East-West convergence as a series of overlapping stages:

1. *First stage—1960-1980.* Ideological conflicts will be deepened internationally, domestically, and within the Soviet Communist party, as the ideological struggles are intensified between Stalinists and Maoists on one hand and realist forces of Leninist communism on the other hand. This process will bring about an ideological victory of realist forces who support the policy of peaceful coexistence and strengthening of democracy and economic reform, through

violent ideological disputes and struggles or perhaps even the introduction of multiparty systems in the Soviet Union and other Socialist countries.

2. *Second stage—1972-1985*. The reformist leftists of the bourgeois class will win a victory in the United States and other capitalist countries by the necessity for social reform and peaceful coexistence and by the pressure from Socialist countries and reformist forces (workers and intelligentsia) within capitalist countries. These leftist reformists will start the program of convergence with socialism, toward worldwide cooperation for social progress and peaceful coexistence and also for a change in the form of ownership. The role of the intellegentsia will increase and racial discrimination and militarism will suffer severe setbacks.

3. *Third stage—1972-1990*. The United States and the Soviet Union will overcome their differences and move to solve the North-South problem. Twenty percent of the tax revenue of advanced nations will be used for that purpose. Industrialization will be promoted, for example, large-scale fertilizer plants and irrigation systems powered by nuclear energy will be constructed in less developed countries. At the same time disarmament will progress.

4. *Fourth stage—1980-2000*. As the result of convergence of the two systems differences of social systems will be reduced. Intellectual freedom and social economic progress will be promoted. The conflicts among the states will be solved and world government will be established. Decisive progress is expected in the field of nuclear energy. Exploration of the universe will be carried out on a large scale.

It is easy to point out rough spots in Sakharov's argument and to criticize its excessive optimism, but these points are not essential. If one sincerely hopes for the disappearance of the difference and subsequently of the confrontation between the two systems in order to achieve stable peace in the world, and if one seeks any possible form for achieving that objective, particularly from the Communist side, Sakharov's concept of the future of the world may be one of the most practical and probable scenarios.

What he expects is violent ideological struggles in the Communist world. In that ideological turmoil he expects reason to prevail, that is, ideological victory of realists who support peaceful coexistence, democracy, and economic reforms. He must have had in mind the model of a society which existed in Czechoslovakia for more than half a year prior to the invasion. Then censorship was virtually abolished and almost complete freedom of expression was realized in Czechoslovakia. Certainly his vision presupposes some degree of freedom of expression and political thought—free enough to assure that reason will prevail.

Concerning Western society, he expects the eventual victory of leftist reformists among workers and the intelligentsia. This does not seem to be an entirely unreasonable expectation. Then he dreams of cooperation of the two worlds in tackling all the problems of the world, and eventually forming a world government.

I would not dismiss the scenario of Sakharov as totally unrealistic. In fact, if the Soviet Union had decided not to invade Czechoslovakia and if "socialism with a human face" had been allowed to proceed in an eternally continuing spring of Prague, the scenario of Sakharov might well have been taken as a proof of fantastic insight, reality far from a dream.

In the true sense of the word the Czechoslovakian invasion of 1968 was historical and far-reaching in its effect. It is a watershed which marked a shift from ideological optimism to cynical realism in the minds of statesmen and academics with the intention of tackling the East-West relation for a stable world peace, and from hope to despair in the minds of people who believed in the inevitable force toward evolution and progress for a better world.

In my original book I expressed sympathy with Sakharov for the possible frustration he may have felt at the Czechoslovakian invasion. According to a recent report his frustration seems to have been beyond my imagination. He is reported to have said that he was somewhat an idealist when he wrote it, since it was before the Czechoslovakian invasion; now he is sadder but wiser; then he called himself a Socialist; now he would like to call himself a liberalist. He concluded his remarks by saying that he was not a pessimist but an inborn optimist, and that he was simply making an objective analysis of the current situation, predicting a dark age of many years to come.

Some Aspects of the Cultural Revolution. The convergence theory is by nature applicable only to advanced countries, and not to countries like the People's Republic of China. Chinese spokesmen in fact have commented on the concept of the convergence theory on very few occasions. All through the cultural revolution, however, the Chinese kept pointing out the danger of the entire Chinese system being changed toward capitalism. The real motive and significance of the cultural revolution is still undetermined. The cultural revolution and incidents which took place during that period undermined China's prestige and image in all countries in the world except two or three, and in the present era of new detente with China the Western nations are polite enough not to open up this old wound. Therefore the cultural revolution still waits for a final assessment in the future. However, there is one salient fact which nobody can deny. In the course of the power struggle during the cultural revolution, whether or not it is related to the cultural revolution itself, Mao won over Liu. And the label put on Liu and all the enemies of the cultural revolution was "the people who are in power taking the capitalist road." It is an approach based on the dynamic element of a society saying that unless something is done the entire system will be swayed toward capitalism.

It is again a curious coincidence that the cultural revolution started in 1966 in the same year the Western detente policy toward Eastern Europe was launched. The two may be related in the sense that both of them are reactions to Khruschevian liberalization and peaceful coexistence in the early 1960s and to the introduction of new economic reform in the Soviet Union in 1965. While Western detente advocates saw a ray of hope in the Russian economic reform, the Chinese must have seen a deadly danger in it.

The *People's Daily Observer* on June 4, 1967 commented:

In the Soviet Union, which is the first Socialist state built by the hand of Lenin himself, the proletariat dictatorship was replaced by bourgeois dictatorship, capitalism revived and the socialist regime faded away . . . Why has the Russian tragedy occurred? The most fundamental lesson is the fact that a proletarian regime was usurped by the revisionist group of Khrushchev. . . . As Chairman Mao pointed out, representatives of bourgeoisie hiding in the party, government, army and cultural circles are anti-revolutionary, revisionist elements. They are waiting for a chance to seize power and replace proletarian dictatorship by bourgeois dictatorship. The Chinese Great Proletarian Cultural Revolution is taking into consideration this serious historical lesson.

Inaccuracy in the usage of words is abundant, as in many Chinese documents during the cultural revolution. The description of bourgeois dictatorship for the present Soviet regime may be just as inaccurate as describing Japan, until quite recently, as being in the stage of the revival of militarism. The entire idea of the cultural revolution itself is hard to explain in the context of historical materialism, for it insists that without repeated spiritual reformation there is a danger of creeping capitalism, with emphasis on the spiritual side rather than on the material side. Discarding all comments on form and logic, we could understand it simply to mean that the power structure will become bureaucratic and corrupted against the interest of people unless spiritual revolution is enforced repeatedly. As a country which has recently succeeded in seizing power, it is wary of the revival of any prerevolutionary tendency. It is not hard to imagine the difficulty the Chinese are facing in eliminating the habit of abuse of the power and corruption of bureaucrats and party officials which have a tradition of thousands of years. This is a case where the Gaullist concept of history and tradition is more applicable than the economic theory of con-vergence. Also we can see an example of the possibility of de-ideologization without any corresponding social or economic revolution.

Future of Liberalization in Communist
States and More Thoughts on
Convergence Policy

Concept of Liberalization. All idealistic approaches to East-West relations antici-pate some metamorphosis in Communist society. In their efforts to find a ray of hope in existing trends in Communist states, the so-called liberalization in the East draws much attention. In fact, the question of liberalization has been continuously and intensively treated by Western scholars and mass media from the middle of the 1950s to the present day.

In the so-called liberalization of the Soviet Union there are three factors which substantially differ from each other in terms of motives and later development.

The first element is de-Stalinization. This includes the motive and effects of Krushchev's criticism of Stalin and the entire proposal for peaceful coexistence, both made at the Twentieth Party Congress in 1956. Domestically it has meant the end of the Stalinist rule of terror. However, the system and practice of judiciary procedure in the Soviet Union is so vastly different from that in Western society that it may be still doubtful if we can define it properly as an "end of the reign of terror" in the sense used in Western societies. One description of Russian society after de-Stalinization which I came across and thought pertinent is that the Russian citizens are no longer afraid of a knock at the door or footsteps outside at midnight. It must have been a tremendous change in the lives of Russian citizens, regardless of the objective standard of human rights now existing in Russian society. In East European countries it meant the recognition of "different roads to socialism" and the possibility of more independent policies, domestically and internationally. It had a far-reaching impact, too, on East-European states, starting with the Poznan incident, then the Hungarian Revolution, and finally the Prague Spring.

We have heard talk of re-Stalinization since the fall of Khrushchev. There is some visible evidence such as the partial restoration of the figure of Stalin himself, the purges of intellectuals, insane asylums, etc., as well as other more sophisticated evidence like the definition of peaceful coexistence. Whether we call it re-Stalinization or de-Khrushchevization, both domestically and internationally, we may safely define the attitude of the present Soviet regime as not so liberal as Khrushchev's regime, although it is far from a return to the Stalinist reign of terror.

The second element is economic reform. It is essentially rationalization of the Soviet economy, a need which increases as the Soviet economy matures. Since this reform tries to achieve its goal partly by eliminating the inefficiency stemming from excessive central control of the economy, it is often called economic liberalization. It was started under the present regime of Brezhnev, parallel with political and ideological de-Khrushchevization, although these cross-currents of liberalization and de-liberalization were often overlooked. So far, this new economic reform seems to have achieved partial success. It has at least created the mood for rationalization which helped to eliminate obviously obsolete and inefficient organization of work. The field to which it has contributed most seems to include those industries which are already modern and efficient. This phenomenon was deftly abstracted by Galbraith as the development of industrial systems as we have seen before. It appears, however, that there is still a long way to go to rationalize the entire economic system of the Soviet Union. If the remaining inefficient part of the Soviet economy were to undermine the entire economic development, as in the case of Czechoslovakia, it would produce a political crisis, or it would at least add to the momentum for some political and social changes. In reality, however, the Soviet economy has succeeded in maintaining, on an average, a higher growth rate than that of the United States, and is not in desperate need of further drastic economic reform, however desirable it may be. As clearly seen in Bregel's view on the convergence theory, the Soviet Union tries to limit economic reform to rationalization strictly within the framework of a Communist state-planned economy. Therefore, we must expect Soviet economic reform or liberalization to progress only as far as the administrative authority desires and to do so without undermining the political and social system of the Soviet Union.

The third element is the movement for intellectual freedom. This started as a result of the government policy of de-Stalinization. It soon departed, however, from the objective and scope of the original government intention and created a political and social problem within the Communist system by its independent development. As far as government policy is concerned, the literary "liberalization" has been in a complete process of retrogression during the last ten years: retrogression which started almost as soon as liberalization took place. The literary thaw started after the death of Stalin in 1953 and was given momentum by Khrushchev's criticism of Stalin in 1956. Already in 1957, however, the Soviet government instituted a campaign against freedom of expression, as a direct result of incidents in Poland and Hungary. And we can see the continuous effort of the Soviet government to try to contain the literary movement under government control all through the remainder of the Khrushchev period. A few weeks after Khrushchev's dismissal from his post as First Secretary of the Party, *Pravda*, on November 1, 1964, editorialized on the concept of "Socialist realism," stressing the tie between people's lives and their responsibility as Russian citizens, and called upon Russian writers to prepare literary monuments for the fiftieth anniversary of the Soviet regime in 1967 and the celebration of Lenin's one hundredth birthday in 1970. Since then the Soviet government has been consistently supporting "Socialist realism," as we have seen in the episodes concerning the repression of Solzhenitzin's and others' literary freedom and Kuznetsov's seeking asylum abroad. The ideological explanation of "Socialist realism" is too complicated for detailed consideration here. The simplest way to grasp the notion is to imagine a painting of a Russian laborer at work, radiant with happiness and pride in being born in the Soviet Union and in being a Soviet worker. Any form of the arts which depicts the other side of human life, particularly in the Soviet Union, may be suspected of being either anti-Socialist or anti-realistic. The control of literary activity by the Brezhnev regime, at the beginning, was not radically different from that in the time of Khrushchev, but since the Czechoslovakian crisis, control started to be tightened further and the resistance of literary circles also became more conspicuous to the outside world.

These three developments of "liberalization" should be treated separately in any detailed analysis. Sometimes there has been a tendency in Japan or elsewhere to expect increasing freedom of expression, or even the possibility of convergence of the political system of both worlds, based on the fact that the Soviet Union launched its economic reform. This kind of short-circuit argument should be carefully avoided, at least in short-term or middle-term analysis. We must also be wary of the tendency to note only the bright side of the reality. It may be possible to produce a theory that Soviet society is inevitably being liberalized, if we ignore the time difference and select the de-Stalinization period of the 50s, economic reforms of the 60s and occasional bursts of anti-establishment literature and essays, discarding the other side of the reality, such as re-Stalinization, anti-convergence arguments and the trend toward stricter control of freedom of expression. Anyone can understand that the theory of inevitable liberalization is out of balance, but we can still find similar arguments quite often in Western journalism.

What then is the chance for a metamorphosis in the Soviet political and social system? All the arguments we have seen are either very vague and in a very long term of historical perspective or they are carefully limited to the possibility of economic convergence, or they fall into a reckless short-circuit argument. In sum, it is hard to expect any significant change in the Soviet political system in a foreseeable future. For example, the introduction of a multiparty system, one of the hallmarks of political change, cannot be foreseen even in Yugoslavia. Djilas, who suggested the introduction of such a multiparty system, was imprisoned. In the short spring of Prague there was a move to restore the activity of Social Democrats, but the Soviet Union vehemently opposed it and the Czechoslovakian government, even before the invasion, did not dare to permit it. Therefore, even if liberalization had proceeded unhampered by the invasion, there would have been little chance for a multiparty system as long as Czechoslovakian development remained under the control of Svoboda and Dubcek. There seems to be an insurmountable limit as long as twentieth century communism holds the banner of Marxism-Leninism, and not that of Marxism alone. It is also doubtful that the Soviet Union might change in the future to adopt a system similar to that of Yugoslavia, considering Lenin's suspicion of trade unions, manifested in his criticism of anarcho-syndicalism.

The remaining possibility may lie in the future of intellectual freedom. As the example of the Prague Spring shows, freedom of expression has the power of undermining the entire political, social, and economic system of a government which has previously enforced an effective control over such expression. When we examine closely the political systems of hundreds of countries in today's world, we wonder how many regimes could survive complete freedom of expression—how many regimes besides the United States, Japan, and other countries with the tradition of Western democracy and pluralism.

On the question of freedom of expression, Lenin also left a negative doctrine.

Perhaps this is a fundamental question in Marxism, dating even before Lenin. I have to request the generosity of readers for my audacity in invading the philosophical field, but since we are talking about the possibility of the convergence of the two systems it does seem necessary to go back to the origin of Marxism. In modern times the target for destruction by all revolutionaries was any tyranny which denied liberty and equality. In subsequent revolutions, the revolutionaries naturally sought liberty and equality, which gradually turned out to be incompatible with each other in the polemics of revolutionary theories in the nineteenth century. Setting aside the argument whether the present Communist regime really achieved at least one of its revolutionary ideals—equality—the question arises whether equality and liberty are compatible in revolutionary theory. Although Bakunin's theory of anarchism was discredited by both Marxists and capitalists, we do see repeated revivals in anarcho-syndicalism during the Russian revolution, and even in the current anti-establishment youth movement everywhere in the world. They are theoretically confused, but from the historical perspective of the conflicts between the two schools of liberty and equality, these anti-establishment movements belong to the former.

Of course there is the argument that even Lenin had in his mind a more idealistic and liberalistic idea, as expressed in *State and Revolution*, and that Lenin's strictures against freedom of criticism were necessary only during the process of revolution and not applicable to postrevolutionary society. It is also a fact that a certain amount of freedom of expression is a welcome thing in any system for a minimum healthy development of the system, like the role of the French intellectual in the period of prerevolutionary absolutism, and enlightened leaders of a system are quite often aware of this fact, however autocratic the system itself may be. In fact much of the advice attributed to Sakharov is really constructive opinion within the framework of the present Communist regime. Brave remarks made by people like Sakharov and Amalrik are the words of patriots, expressing concern for the future of the Slavic peoples. Furthermore, we have to remember the greatness of the Russian literary tradition. Some people cite the lack of democratic tradition in Russian history as a reason for pessimism about any political metamorphosis, in comparison with East European nations which experienced democracy before the Russian invasion. These conclude that some form of authocracy is inevitable in Russia. In Communist China, we constantly see the old China, with its tradition of three thousand years of civilization, everywhere beneath the Communist system which has been imposed, and we consider it a source of possible future change. Comparing Russian history with Chinese we are conscious of its brevity. However nobody can deny that Russia has one of the greatest literary traditions of the modern world, which is not only deep and superb in its quality, but has consistently expressed humanism fearlessly even in the time of czarist autocracy. It may be one of the greatest potential forces for evolution in Russian society.

It is understandable that all the hopes and frustrations of idealistic people revolve around the question of freedom of expression in the Communist countries. Since both the governing elites and the people supporting reforms understand fully the utmost significance of intellectual freedom in Russia, the only practical prediction I could possibly make at this moment is that this question of intellectual liberty will travel a long, zig-zag course in the foreseeable future.

Incidentally, literal application of convergence to intellectual freedom might well mean a mutual approach with the Russians liberalizing expression while the Western nations tighten control over it. It is the world described by George Orwell in 1984. We can recall abundant examples since the interwar period of countries with fragile internal political bases under severe attack from Communist propaganda. The government must enforce a tighter control on freedom of expression as a defensive measure. This is a tendency not for convergence or mutual understanding, but for confrontation and fascism. From this we must conclude, as far as intellectual freedom is concerned, that the Western world has to insist on unilateral liberalization on the Communist side.

In the effort to grasp the vague notion of so-called detente diplomacy, we have at least witnessed one set of ideas put together as a policy of the Western world vis-à-vis the Communist world in the particular period between 1966 and the Czechoslovakian invasion. In short, the Western side sought something beyond mere peaceful coexistence in that period. It sought not only a condition where peace is maintained but also something new, which might give hope for a more lasting peace based on the mutual reduction of fundamental differences which separate the two systems. In the same period the Soviet Union consistently maintained that peaceful coexistence is the only principle to govern relations between the East and West. In the more erratic Khrushchevian period, peaceful coexistence itself often meant something more than a mere maintenance of the peace, but the Brezhnev regime is applying a more strict interpretation of this principle. If we define Western detente policy as that entire area of Western approach which goes beyond the limit of the Soviet definition of peaceful coexistence, then from the Russian position that area must be considered capitalist propaganda. From the Communist point of view, it is nothing more than propaganda that nationalistic and humanistic elements are superior to ideology or that both economic systems will eventually converge into a new mixed system. In that period, therefore, the Soviet Union was always defensive on the issue of detente, just as the Western world was always defensive on the issue of peaceful coexistence in the period of Khruschev, considering it mainly Communist propaganda.

It is certainly true that at one time the Western side was swayed by idealism and by optimistic assessment of the situation which was better suited for idealism. One of the faults of the convergence theory is that it posited the inevitability as well as the desirability of progress in all societies. Westerners underestimated the fact that, for any system, survival is an imperative, while progress is a matter of choice—one *could* do without it.

A friend of mine who twice lived in the Soviet Union told me that he was deeply impressed by the remarkable improvement in the ordinary citizen's life in the USSR during Khrushchev's time, and that he was again surprised quite recently by the fact that there was so very little further improvement in the years since then. In Communist states, statistics are not always reliable and the actual experiences of a foreign inhabitant there may quite often tell the truth. According to my friend's explanation, this may be partly attributable to Soviet efforts, after the lesson they learned in the Cuban crisis, to reach a parity with the United States by building 1,000 intercontinental nuclear missiles in ten years.

The Chinese case may be more obvious. According to one assessment, China's economic growth for the ten years between 1958 and 1968 was virtually zero, yet in that same period, which included the famine of 1960-61 and the confusion of the cultural revolution, China succeeded in becoming a nuclear power. The fact that a regime or system survived zero growth for ten years, while almost all other major powers doubled or tripled their national income in the same period, will confound any believer in the theory that economic development or failure is bound to affect a political system.

The fundamental problem of the convergence theory is that it tacitly presupposes that economic evolution will eventually affect the political system. It is Marxist theory which contends that the economic base decides the political superstructure. The convergence theory may have simply or diplomatically accommodated itself to the Communist premise. I personally doubt seriously if twentieth century communism and the revolution it has achieved is based on economic evolution rather than a political development.

In reality, political decisions can do anything. The Soviet Union could destroy the result of an accumulation of ten years gradual development in Czechoslovakia with the blitzkrieg of one day. If ten years' evolution can be reversed by a simple political decision, the convergence theory amounts to the suggestion that one build a castle of sand on a rough beach.

Since the Czechoslovakian invasion the atmosphere has changed. Now the Western side knows that economic and social evolution are at the mercy of political and ideological decision, that the invincibility of nationalism is a myth, that the East European countries would never go beyond the point which the Soviets allow, and that the expression of humanity can be controlled by domestic administrative measures.

Renewed efforts to achieve East-West detente by the Nixon administration and Brandt administration are based on this reality. They know that, in East European affairs, they can go only so far as the Soviet will accept and, therefore, they have concentrated on dealings with the Soviets. In that sense, the detente in 1966 was based on idealism and optimism, and today on cynical realism.

In 1966, de-ideologization meant gradual progress of both systems, gradual reduction of the differences between them, more emphasis on common human values and eventual development of mutual understanding. Nowadays, de-ideologization means putting ideology in abeyance, stressing the naked reality of world politics, i.e., power politics. One cannot deny that one effective method of de-ideologization is simply to forget about ideology. If the Christian world had not cared how badly Moslems treated Christian pilgrims in Jerusalem, there would have been no Crusades. They would have had peaceful coexistence based on balance of power and mutual negligence, although it may have been too bad for the Christians in Jerusalem. A similar situation seems to exist in the present world. Quite recently Sakharov is reported to have said, "The situation has further deteriorated since the visit of President Nixon.... Russian authority became more impudent. They think that Western public opinion, because of the detente, no longer cares about the miserable conditions in the Soviet Union.... Never before has our movement been in such difficulty as at present." Detente based on cynical realism is a betrayal of the idealists inside the iron curtain. I also remember that American anti-establishment people were furious at the Russians for accepting the presidential visit to Moscow in spite of the renewed bombing of North Vietnam and the mining of Haiphong harbor. A similar situation may exist among Japanese leftists who have opposed the U.S.-Japan security treaty, who must now face the fact that Peking no longer cares about the continuance of the treaty between Japan and the United States.

Still, the detente policy of 1966 and that of today may be the same thing. Even in 1966-1968 realistic thinkers and practitioners in the West never expected anything more than such peaceful coexistence as the Soviet Union wanted to maintain. In any case, we could not possibly have got an inch more in face of the stern Soviet attitude. On the other hand, even in a strictly defined peaceful coexistence, both sides should always be wary of the weakening of the security-mindedness of their own side. The more realistic one is, the more concerned one is to try to maintain the solidarity and preparedness of one's own side and to take one's opponent off guard. In this sense one has to think about development beyond the original scope of peaceful coexistence. Moreover, even realists should know very well that time, particularly a long period of peace, itself has the function of changing things. Negligence of ideological aspects and stress on power politics may also be one of the shortcuts to the burial of ideology and the expression of humanistic and nationalistic sentiment and then on to a gradual change in the Communist system. In that sense, detente based on cynical realism is not different at all from that based on idealism and optimism. The only difference is whether one talks about a possible future or simply remains silent.

In any case, detente policy is a game, in which each side competes to see which will survive better in peace and mutual contact. The word "peace" can be replaced by "low tension." We have always thought that a totalitarian regime needs more high tension and isolation than our free society in order to hold its system together, and therefore we have a definite advantage in the game of surviving in a period of low tension and mutual exchanges. In fact, this must have been part of the reason behind the Western offensive in detente policy. Here again, however, we cannot be categorical about cause and effect relations. We have seen that the Soviet Union and China can be flexible and reasonable in their external affairs and at the same time rigid in domestic affairs, though I do not think that the external and internal policies of Communist countries were necessarily correlated in terms of flexibility and rigidity, even in the past. I do feel there has been a tendency to increase separation of these two facets. Perhaps people are becoming more realistic and therefore care less about the logical contradictions of what they do in different places, but more about what they find necessary or expedient to do on each occasion. We may pretend to ignore ideology or we may be truly getting tired of ideology, but Communist ideological education has been rather intensified in the past years, not only in China under the cultural revolution and after, but also in Russia.

If we look into the intensity of Socialist education in these countries, we can only become doubtful about the inevitability of a decline of ideology. Millions of youths are still inculcated with Marxist-Leninist theses, which continue to assert stridently the necessity of world revolution and the possibility of war with capitalism. And he who learns these principles well becomes a youth activist and eventually part of the party cadre. It would not be surprising at all if we were to experience, in the future, a new surge of ideological passion in the Communist countries, with considerable effect on East-West relations.

Therefore, nothing is certain about the future of Communist society, its political system, its relation with the Western world, and the future of the world in terms of the differences between the two systems.

So what is left as solid fact to rely upon after all these analyses? One is peaceful coexistence in the strictest sense of the word, that is, the impossibility of total nuclear war under present mutual nuclear deterrence. Nothing is yet certain enough to lessen the importance of the deterrence system. The other reality is the system of our own. The Communist system may or may not change. If it changes the real motive may be economic, nationalistic, or humanistic, or simply because of the lapse of time. But anything in their control is uncertain, while that in our control is certain or, at least, can be maintained and improved by our efforts. One thing is clear in East-West relations: that we have to compete with each other over which system is more attractive for the people of the two systems. Propaganda cannot eventually win when it is exposed to reality long enough. It is not only peaceful competition proposed by Khrushchev on economic affairs, but it is an overall race including the standards of human rights and intellectual freedom. As long as we are able to believe in the superiority of our political, economic, social, and moral system, we will feel we have the East-West relation under control. We might conclude that such a race is more fruitful for the future of mankind than the cold war or mere peaceful coexistence.

4 Japanese Peace Diplomacy

Framework of Diplomacy

Postwar Japanese diplomacy has been defined as "peace diplomacy" for constitutional and other reasons. It is supposed not only to be peaceful in itself and hopeful that the international environment is peaceful, but also to do its utmost to contribute to the peace of the whole world.

What then should Japanese diplomacy do for the peace of the world? What can it do? In examining the possibility of Japanese peace diplomacy, first we should know the nature of diplomatic policy itself.

Foreign Policy

Diplomatic policy or foreign policy is, by nature, different from the policy of other administrative branches of the government, because it has other governments or nations to deal with. For example, the significance of policy planning is almost decisive in the case of administration for public works. It can decide how many bridges should be built in one fiscal year and after appropriate financial arrangements are made, the bridges are built. In the case of foreign policy on the other hand, a policy duly adopted by a government and by the will of the people, and also with all the financial and physical means necessary for it, may not be executed at all because it depends upon the attitude of other parties and conditions then prevailing in the international picture.

There are innumerable examples in history in which the diplomacy of a small power proved ineffectual in the face of the force of a big power. I might again quote the example of Czechoslovakia in 1968. The diplomacy which the Czechoslovakian government conducted in 1968 could be described as perfect. In its negotiation with the Soviet Union, Czechoslovakian diplomacy in the spring of 1968 was perfectly correct and proper and explained its position in a very logical way. The government and people cooperated with one another so that there was no provocative act or even an accident affecting the Russian soldiers, who were then stationed there under the name of maneuvers. It succeeded in realizing the withdrawal of the Russian troops through difficult negotiations which ended in the Conference at Bratislava. All the newspapers and comments in the world unsparingly applauded the success of Czechoslovakian diplomacy. They thought it was a perfect success, and so did the citizens

79

of Prague. For 20 days, until this success was suddenly terminated by invasion, it was reported that citizens of Prague talked, danced, embraced, and cried, day and night, with whomever they encountered. Looking back on the history of that incident I cannot find a single fault in the diplomatic conduct of the Czechoslovakian government, except that it did not have the right party to deal with.

This was an extreme case, but in day-to-day foreign affairs there are also many examples in which things did not work out as Japan had hoped. Projects which were obviously beneficial for Japan and the other party failed in execution or were postponed because of various domestic and international circumstances. In some cases a project which would have unilaterally benefited the other party failed to be realized, as in the case of economic and technical assistance to a developing country.

It is true that today's Japan does carry some weight on the international scene. Japan is now the third largest economic power in the world and its economy still expands at a rate faster than that of any other major economic power. Apart from straight-line projections which suggest a fantastic economic future for Japan, it is undeniable that Japanese stature and Japan's voice in world affairs will grow as its economy grows. However, we have to suppress the optimism which suggests that Japan by itself might influence the trend of the world in certain directions which Japan might prefer. Even in the purely economic field, in which Japan is likely to exercise its largest influence, Japan, which now produces less than one-tenth of the world's gross national product, will not always be able to influence the remaining 90 percent of the world, unless it effectively combines its strength with that of other major economic powers. Therefore the importance to Japan of economic cooperation with the United States, which contributes about 30 percent to the world's GNP, is obvious for Japan even in this abstract context. The Japanese voice in world affairs concerning the question of peace and security will be far smaller than the percentage expressed iterms of its GNP. The late Prime Minister Ikeda, who marked his administration with his exclusive emphasis on the economic growth of Japan in the first half of the 1960s, is reported to have stated, after his visit to Great Britain, that his voice would have been ten times bigger than its present one had Japan possessed military capability. In the question of peace and war, the Japanese voice will be smaller than that of the People's Republic of China all through the 1970s. On the question of local conflicts controllable by U.N. actions, the Japanese voice will be even smaller than nations like India or Sweden, which have the capability to dispatch military personnel for peace-keeping or military observation operations. (It is the policy of the Japanese government not to send any defense units for overseas operations, even for noncombatant peace-keeping operations.)

I do not discuss the merit or demerit of this Japanese policy. I simply point it out as a fact of life. We should have no illusions about Japanese influence on world peace and security. Some people think Japan should exert a unique influence in international affairs by upholding its principle of absolute pacifism, but we have little evidence to believe the world recognizes any special "historical mission" of Japan. It may sometimes happen that an innocent foreign observer accommodates to this Japanese pretension for diplomatic or other reasons, but once a nation faces a question which concerns its own security, priority to that Japanese pretension will be given a low place.

Another pretension often suggested in the late 1960s was that Japan should play a role in the peace settlement in Vietnam, given its sincerity in the cause of peace and its uncommitted position on either side of the Vietnam question. North Vietnam did not pay much attention to various suggestions or proposals for a Vietnam peace settlement; according to some calculations there were more than fifty of them, mostly made by nonaligned Asian and African nations—and decided to hold direct negotiations with the United States and South Vietnam. Any efforts by Japan would have elicited the same reaction from North Vietnam as did all other proposals of the kind. It is irrelevant whether Japan was pro-American, pro-Chinese, nonaligned, or peace-loving. Unless Japan could be responsible for the execution of the agreed settlement and was ready and able to enforce it upon both parties with effective means, it was only natural for North Vietnam to prefer to deal directly with the United States and South Vietnam.

Analysis and Future Prospect. The fact that foreign policy is very much at the mercy of circumstances emphasizes the importance of analysis and predictions for the international situation. Analysis is an effort to know what the current situation is and predictions, of course, are a projection of what's likely to happen in the future. Since Japan is not an overwhelming world power, such as the United States was right after the Second World War, Japanese foreign policy should seek its national interest and national objective within limits, sometimes taking advantage of the existing international situation and future trends, rather than setting up an a priori national objective and expecting an ideal form of international society suited to that objective. Therefore, realistic analysis and future prospect should always have precedence over policy.

Analysis is important professional work for any foreign service. The Japanese foreign ministry analyzes the situation and draws up future prospects every day, every week, every month, and every year, discusses them, compares them with the assessment of other sources, and revises them according to the ever-changing international situation. I personally believe such work is quite satisfactory and useful for the purpose, although it is always with the reservation " . . . unless an unexpected situation arises."

Being conscious of a slight digression, I should like to go a little further into the matter of analysis. I experienced a few "unexpected situations" during the period when I was in charge of analysis. Who expected the cultural revolution in China at the beginning of 1966? Nobody among the China experts of the entire world. A very few predicted the Russian invasion into Czechoslovakia in 1968, particularly after the Bratislava Conference, but nobody, as far as I remember, among the experts, journalists, or commentators in Japan. The Tet offensive in the same year was undoubtedly the top military secret of North Vietnam and the Vietcong, and unpredictable by its very nature. While few expected an attack of that kind, still less did they expect the far-reaching impact it had on the American policy which followed it.

It is true that some people are entitled to say that they knew, but after reviewing their reasoning there are more elements of coincidence on this or that particular occasion than realistic assessment of the prevailing situation. Nationalist Chinese sources were forever hopeful of internal confusion and dissension on the Mainland. Yugoslavian papers were ever watchful of Soviet actions with maximum wariness. Some people always believed that a war of "people's liberation" was invincible and that the United States was bound to withdraw sooner or later. All these standing predictions could secure a one-in-ten-year success, but achieve a very low batting average in day-to-day analysis.

It may sound paradoxical, but well thought-out analysis is necessary for contingencies where these unexpected situations arise. It is like a game of bridge. The position of the ace of trumps may not be detectable even after taking into consideration all the available signs. In that case the probability is fifty-fifty for everybody, expert or not. It may even happen that a person who relies on "card sense" may do better than one who studies through all the available possibilities. In case of failure in locating the ace of trumps, however, an expert then has a much clearer picture of all the remaining hands and may be able to find a rare chance for recovery, while an amateur is still walking in the dark. Of course, in many cases the success or failure of a particular hand depends so much on locating the particular ace that there is no practical difference between expert and amateur, but in the long run an expert has more probability of success in assessing the situation correctly. This is a defensive argument for us professionals. I might give as an example President Johnson's announcement that he would halt the bombing of North Vietnam on March 31, 1968. The president's announcement had tremendous impact all over East and Southeast Asia. People who believed in the invincibility of a people's liberation war and had predicted eventual American defeat were triumphant and expected that North Vietnam, which was so strategically superior to the United States, would not accept the negotiations and would put further military pressure on the South, while most practitioners thought it must have been a gesture already anticipating a favorable response from North Vietnam. The result was obvious in the favorable response of North Vietnam only a few days later. Of course, however, to the public eyes and in a larger political framework it was they, the believers in the eventual defeat of the United States, who had correctly located the ace of trumps.

In any case, accuracy of assessment and future prospects made by foreign affairs experts is a matter of probability and is also subject to constant modification, revision, and even reversal. Since foreign policy is subject to ever changing circumstance, it is also under constant modification and revision. One Japanese foreign minister, when asked the question "What is the fundamental principle of diplomacy?" replied, "to act case by case." According to General De Gaulle, things change constantly and there is no such thing as an eternal truth. These words reveal some fundamentals about diplomacy.

The policy planning function of foreign affairs has received some attention in foreign offices in the United States, Great Britain, Germany, the Soviet Union, and also Japan in the postwar years, but there is not yet a clear assessment as to which administrative branch should carry out this particular purpose. What policy planners do at this moment is to hold a kind of brainstorming exercise to analyze a situation, plan a policy, and discuss it. One policy planner in the State Department even said that the purpose of policy planning was not to make policy but to stimulate discussion by inviting comments on draft policy. This may be a practical concept of policy planning in foreign affairs.

Political Environment of the World

Since analysis and future prospects should have precedence over policy, we should look into the future of world environment before discussing Japanese diplomacy. Also, for the purpose of this book, the prospects for the future have to cover a certain length of time, say ten years or to the end of the 1970s. Usually practitioners avoid making predictions more than six months ahead. For the needs of current policy planning, however, it is quite often required to cover one to two years.

A one to two year period is the most challenging time length for any realistic analysis; beyond that analysis mainly belongs to the field of historical philosophy. For example, the Sino-Soviet dispute started in the middle 1950s and became conspicuous early in the 1960s, but it was not perceived by the shrewdest observers until the end of the 1950s. Some people hopefully predicted the so-called Tito-ization of China at the time of the Communist take-over in 1949, considering the long historical independence of the Chinese nation. At that time, it was impossible to predict the present ideological disputes at the beginning of the 1950s. Dating back ten years further, 1940 was one year before the outbreak of the Pacific war and only God knew what would happen ten years later.

We should assume now that for this decade the interrelationships among the United States, the Soviet Union, and China will decide the fundamental structure of the world situation. Particularly for Japan, these three powers have overwhelming importance, since European influence in East Asia has not been felt much since the last war. Ten years, however, is too long a period to expect a stable trend of interrelationship among the three powers. We have to be prepared for some reversals and re-reversals of friendly or antagonistic relations among these three powers during the decade. Already since I wrote this in my original book in 1970, there has been a rather significant reversal in U.S.-China relations. The trilateral relation was and is unpredictable when discussed in a time frame of more than one to two years.

A more constructive result can be achieved by analyzing and considering the prospects of the political and economic future of these three powers. I do not assert that the domestic condition of a country always decides its foreign policy, but certainly domestic conditions do set a large framework for the activity of the country in external affairs. Here is one reason that the interrelationship among the Western nations, including the United States, Western European countries, and Japan, are more predictable than the above trilateral relationship, because we can assume, with a reasonably high degree of probability, that free democratic institutions, both political and economic, will remain constant in these countries in this decade and will support the fundamental cooperative relationship among these countries.

Let us begin by examining the Communist states. One reason to begin at this point is that in the postwar period there were more cases where the Communist side took the initiative in international affairs and the Western side reacted to it rather than vice-versa, in spite of, or because of, the strategic supremacy always maintained by the Western side. So it is practical to examine the Communist side first. Another reason is that analysis of Communist states is already an established field in international affairs and, moreover, that such analysis suffered serious revisions because of the cultural revolution or Czechoslovakian invasion, thus discouraging immature, simplistic or over-optimistic arguments, while many arguments concerning the future of the United States or Japan are still quite experimental.

Russia. Based on what we have seen, it may be possible to draw a schematic picture of Russian society after the death of Stalin. Russia is still in a long process of the change from Stalin's era, characterized by the strict regimentation not only of its own citizens but also that of the forces of the international Communist movement. It is also characterized by massive concentration on heavy industry at the expense of the living standard of its people. There exist various trends of so-called liberalization, such as de-Stalinization, economic reform, or peaceful coexistence, whose origin, timing, and objectives may from time to time differ. When these trends seem in the eyes of the Soviet leaders to be having unfavorable effects on the Soviet system or on Russia's national interest, then Soviet authorities try to control the trend. We may call this the zig-zag phenomenon of Soviet liberalization.

We expect that this zig-zag movement will continue to exist all through the 1970s. The question is how strong the internal pressure is for liberalization and to what extent Soviet leaders will or can control it. Among experts opinions differ on this point. I personally feel that we should not overestimate the pressure for liberalization from within Russian society. I would rather define the Soviet Union as a status quo power. The Soviet Union gained victory in the Second World War, expanded its own territory and its sphere of influence; its living standard is the highest ever. Compared with the Western nations and Japan, the living standard of its people may still seem unsatisfactory, but a great majority of its people do not know the situation abroad and they only know that their living standard is much better than in any period in the past, which means better than in the czarist or Stalinist eras. Therefore we may assume a majority of its people also want the status quo to be maintained. In spite of the obvious necessity for economic reforms we can find no evidence that a majority of Russia's people are pressing for fundamental reform which might even touch the basis of its system.

A fundamental change might happen only when a majority of Russia's leaders and people feel they cannot go on any more under the existing system. This depends on the future development of the Russian economy, in comparison with the economic growth of the capitalist world, and also on the degree of the exposure of its people to the outside world. Even in the worst case, however, Russian leaders would still possess the alternative of creating external tension in order to perpetuate their system. In any case, the evolution of the Russian political, economic, and social condition is extremely slow, and we have good reason to believe that the situation in the Soviet Union will be very like the present one even at the end of the 1970s.

China. We can also see a zig-zag tendency in the policy of the People's Republic of China. The pendulum swung in the past from putting the main emphasis on peaceful coexistence and subsidiary emphasis on the people's liberation struggle to the reverse of this emphasis in external affairs, and from an attitude of economic rationalism and compromise to spiritualism, regimentation, and purge in domestic affairs.

The last half of the 1960s was the period in which stress on the people's liberation struggle in external affairs and on ideology and purge in domestic affairs was carried to an extreme in China. It was therefore expected that the pendulum would swing back sooner or later. At least the first few years of the 1970s were expected to be marked by a trend of growing moderation.

China has, however, many more elements which make the prospect for the future uncertain. We can define Russia as a status quo power with certain achieved stability as a result of its fifty-year history since the revolution. China may be at the stage of prewar Russia, in which it needed collectivization and massive purges to build socialism, although I feel this is an oversimplified application of the Soviet model of history to China. On the other hand, China seems to be under constant inner pressure to regress to her prerevolutionary status, according to the definition Chinese themselves made during the cultural revolution. Therefore, while recognizing the zig-zag tendency as a historical fact of the past twenty years, we do not yet know the overall tendency of the straight line after adjusting for seasonal fluctuations. Moreover, there is real difficulty in determining the historical forces which motivate every turning point of zig-zag evolution. While Russian evolution may be marked by the philosophy or personal tendency of its leader, which of course reflects the need of the era, for example, change from Stalin to Khrushchev and from Khrushchev to Brezhnev, the Chinese evolution, including the cataclysmic Great Leap and cultural revolution and also rapproachement with the United States, have been directed by the same person, Mao Tse-tung. This tremendous personal influence makes it hard to judge the historical necessity or inevitability of these zig-zags and also to predict the future of Chinese society, which depends upon the future decision of Mao as long as he stays, and which has to navigate in unchartered seas without Mao. Therefore, China's future is unpredictable in any case. Taking a ten-year period from now, we cannot exclude the possibility of several years of reasonable economic growth and accumulation of economic power, which can be used for military or other purposes to expand Chinese interest, although the aggregate power of China will continue far smaller than that of the United States or the USSR. In the past example, after a period of comparatively smooth economic growth, China tended to use the power thus gained for adventurous policies, such as the Great Leap or the cultural revolution, rather than initiating a moderate policy and enjoying the peaceful life. We have to admit that so-called trial and error of China was repeated more often than outside observers had expected. Even from the one sure prospect that China will be a full-fledged nuclear power with a few effective ICBMs in the 1970s, one may draw two different conclusions; China might adopt the principle of peaceful coexistence of the Russian type, or it might put a renewed emphasis on local people's liberation struggles with a sufficient deterrent capability against an overall nuclear war. In any case the domestic scene in China will remain overwhelmingly decisive in the future course of Chinese foreign policy.

The United States. The prospect in the coming decade for the United States depends on an assessment of the general trend of American public opinion and the policy reflecting it—above all, the Nixon doctrine, in the late 1960s and the beginning of the 1970s. The focal point is whether we should explain these trends from the traditional elements which have always existed in American politics and political thought, or understand them as an entirely new phenomenon. Once the question is raised in this way, the answer is obvious for anybody; the truth lies in between. Then the real problem is where to find the middle point. According to the cyclical theory, American history experiences alternately a period in which it is full of aspiration, idealism, and impetuosity for solving international or domestic problems, and a subsequent period in which it enjoys a stable, isolated American life. Particularly in this century, Democratic administrations which were marked by the world wars and the New Deal are considered to belong to the former, and the Republic administrations to the latter. If we apply this theory to present American politics, we may consider that the Nixon Administration is a product of the current American trend which is tired of the active and evangelistic Kennedy and Johnson administrations, which tried to solve the fundamental problems of American society, i.e., racial discrimination, and also tried to terminate the Vietnam War by massive intervention. Therefore we should expect at least the several early years of the 70s as a conservative period, yet also a period preparing for a new active phase in the future.

I believe that this cyclical way of thinking must be fundamentally correct. This theory serves to give more historical perspective and prevent us from making the mistake of adopting an abstract and deterministic concept, such as "the era of the United States has gone." We must not underestimate the overwhelming potentialities of the United States, being still by far the strongest nation in the world, and the possibility of America coming back in the world scene with a new vitality in the future.

There may also be new elements. For example, the time has gone when the United States had a large surplus in its trade balance and could use it in any way it liked for executing its external policy. This fact may constitute a new limitation at a time when the United States might prefer active intervention in international affairs in future. Also we do not yet know the final form of reconsolidation of American society, particularly on the question of race and youth. On the other hand, international circumstances would not allow the United State to go back to the isolationism of the 1930s. And we notice the long trend of maturity of American intellectuals, from an abstract to a realistic way of thinking.

So, what needs to be modified in the cyclical theory may be no more than its amplitude. While a conservative, isolationist trend may be inevitable, the amplitude may be limited by the fact that it will be more selective and realistic. And with some audacity we might predict the amplitude of the subsequent active period will be also limited by various circumstances.

Japan and Sino-Soviet Relations. What is the policy implication of the above analysis for Japanese diplomacy? The entire purpose of the above is just to introduce a way of thinking in the analysis of international affairs. While it is obvious that future international circumstances will largely depend upon the attitude of these three countries, the situation of each of these three countries develops according to the unique historical circumstance of each. They do not move fast enough nor in a certain direction as some idealists or intensely policy-minded people hope for. Neither is the USSR walking on the straight road to liberalization and convergence as the idealists hope, nor is the United States heading toward disintegration as some left-wing radicals in the Western world predict—this is the important background factor which must be kept in mind.

The interrelations among the three countries always have the possibility of moving faster than their domestic determinants. Even the Sino-Soviet relation, which appears to be decisively bad at this moment, might change. What is important for Japan is to watch the situation with the utmost attention, preparing for a change which might go beyond the normal framework of the present prospect for future Sino-Soviet relations. Two situations go beyond the normal prospect; reversion to the monolithism of the 1950s and a total Sino-Soviet war. It is obvious that a complete Sino-Soviet rapprochement would change the world power balance fundamentally, just by recalling the impact produced by the Sino-Soviet rift. For Japan, even apart from its political impact, we should recall that the large expansion of Sino-Japanese trade all through the 60s was primarily owing to the Sino-Soviet rift. In case of total war, we have to prepare for a sudden change in the balance of power in the Far East, if the war is conducted effectively in a short period. If the war is prolonged, the position of Japan, the greatest industrial nation in that region, will become delicate and the focus of attention of the nations concerned.

Again this prospect itself has very little significance. Fortunately this section has not so far needed substantial revision since it was originally written three years ago. But it may become suddenly obsolete tomorrow, if, for example, a world war breaks out. The practice of shedding all naive expectations and of being constantly prepared to revise or even reverse existing assessments is the basic requirement for diplomacy in this ever-changing world.

The Basic Diplomatic Work

As we have seen, it never happens that national interests of two sovereign states completely coincide with each other. Frictions and tensions arising out of differences are inevitable even between the most friendly nations. As we may be able to define diplomacy as the art of preventing or minimizing these frictions between states, so we may also say that the relaxation of tension is the objective of diplomacy itself.

Balance of Interest Among Nations

International detente, a more stable structure for lasting peace or any kind of peace, should be built on a certain balance in relations among nations and states, as long as mankind does not possess an effective supranational authority and the world consists of sovereign nations. The basic structure for peace should be based on international relations in which conflicts among national interests are settled on fair and equitable bases. A situation in which one nation gains unbalanced advantage over another nation, even if it is a result of an act of self-sacrifice of the latter, would not last long and would eventually undermine the friendly relation between the two nations. The balance of national interests has a supreme importance in relations between nations.

The element of power also comes in. A relation which was once reasonable between a big power and a small power is not necessarily reasonable when the small country improves its power and stature. The terms of the Versailles Treaty may have been extremely hard on Germany, but as a condition of defeat Germany had no choice but to accept it. Many inequities of the treaty became conspicuous as Germany recovered its power. Although the circumstance is quite different, the Okinawa reversion may have reflected the evolution of a quarter century following the Japanese defeat, during which Japan has become the second largest economic power in the free world and has become ready to assume increasing degrees of international responsibilities.

Balance of interests among states cover wide areas. Beginning with the highly political question of political boundaries and diplomatic recognition, they cover all the fields of security, commerce, investment, fishery, navigation, immigration, cultural exchanges, and so on. In these practical affairs, we try to find common interests to reach reasonable points of compromise which can best accommodate the national interest of both parties and then execute agreements of both parties in good faith.

Some might question whether it is possible for Japan to find a common interest and build a balanced cooperative relation with a Communist state, such as the Soviet Union or China, in spite of the differences in political system or even in spite of the lack of sufficient mutual understanding or trust. Of course it is possible. The effort of constant adjustment of national interests in practical matters is no less important in dealing with countries of different systems than with non-Communist countries. Answers to reverse cases are more obvious. Frictions and even wars between countries of the same system or even the same race are numerous. Hatred between similar races or countries of similar religion often take much more violent forms. Civil wars are the most intense. In general only long-term relations are affected by ideology, stages of economic development, racial and historical similarities. Normal short-term states' relations are affected by more immediate practical national interests. The growth of Sino-Japanese trade before the diplomatic normalization is a good example. Japan became the biggest trade partner of China simply because of Japanese superior economic and technological capability and Japan's geographical advantage, combined with the bad relations of China with the Soviet Union. No historical or macroscopic element helped this growth of Sino-Japan trade since 1963. The same may be said about Japan-Taiwan trade after the normalization. The relation achieved between Russia and Japan is the result of hard-bargaining and compromise on trade, air transportation, fishery, and so on. In dealing with the practical problems between states, the differences of ideology and system count very little. If there is any political problem in trade and other relations with

China, it comes from the fact that another government is in a conflicting position over the legitimate title of China. It is true that, in this sense, in the process of practical adjustment of needs of interests with China, Japan has an extraneous element with which to deal. It is not, however, necessarily related to the fact that China is a Communist country. Similar problems of rivalry exist in the practical business relations of Israel with Arab states.

As the international situation changes, we cannot preclude a situation in which common political interests develop between Japan and a Communist country. Already the Russian papers are attacking "Sino-Japanese collaboration" and the Chinese papers are attacking "Russo-Japanese collaboration," thus counting on the possibility that this kind of political move will happen. For example, with a further deterioration in Sino-Soviet relations, Russia or China might act beyond the political framework it has so far imposed on itself. I do not know whether I should leave the above observation still in the future tense after the events which took place in 1971 and 1972, but I would rather leave it as it is while the form of Sino-Japanese or Russo-Japanese cooperation is still in the process of formation and its future is still uncertain. We do not yet know if the world situation is finally moving toward de-ideologization and will have the multilateral power balance as its only basic structure.

In this book I have no intention of dealing with the multilateral economic questions, which now occupy so much attention in the external affairs of each advanced country, since the purpose here is primarily to examine the relation between Communist and non-Communist states and these multilateral economic relations are mainly among advanced Western nations. I simply wish to point out their importance to the prosperity and solidarity of the Western democracies which form the basis of long-term East-West relations. Furthermore, supposing a de-ideologized world, economic competition or competition for survival, if it comes to a competition for essential material resources, is the greatest cause of international conflicts as we have seen in the example of the 1930s. In that sense multilateral adjustment of economic interests among the advanced nations has a far-reaching bearing on the future peace of the world.

The question of economic assistance, although it is a field in which Japan could and should assume large responsibility, is also beyond the scope here, since it primarily concerns itself with the relation between developed and less developed countries (LDC). In some stage of the cold war there was a time when the bulk of the substance of the North-South problem was said to be the East-West competition in this less developed part of the world. But in fact, economic assistance to the LDC never went beyond the peripheral problem in the context of East-West conflicts, and I believe the question of economic assistance should be judged on its own merits for better economic and political relations between advanced and less developed countries. Also although there was a time when the North-South problem was considered the pressing problem for world peace, there is a tendency nowadays to consider relations among advanced countries more important. In fact its bearing on the peace of the world is in still longer terms than economic relations among the advanced states mentioned in the paragraph above. Here I simply wish to draw attention to a misconception about the effect of economic assistance similar to that about the detente policy. It is true that the domestic social and economic stability of a LDC is a prerequisite for its stable relations with the outside world and that economic assistance is expected to help a less developed country achieve stabilization of its economy and society. However, we cannot be too simplistic about the interrelations among the living standards, social stability, political, and economic system and finally the external policy of a country. It may be true that citizens of a nation with a per capita national income of 2,000 dollars are already status quo minded and have too much to lose in a revolution or a war. But the development from today's 100 dollar per capita standard in China and other parts of Asia to a 2,000 dollar standard is the history of Japan itself from the Meiji Restoration up to now. Looking back into the various political, social, and economic phases we have passed through in the last 100 years, there is no assurance that the progress of economic development in each country to that high standard will take a straight line toward increasing prosperity, stability, and peace. We must reject the myth that every 10 dollars added to per capita national income means added stability and peace. Of course, it is also true that over a very long term there is no other way of achieving the peace and stability of the world except to secure a high reasonable standard of living for all the people of the world. Therefore we should bear in mind that it is a long, long process and does not allow any short-term optimism, but it is a right policy for the future of mankind.

The United Nations and Disarmament

The United Nations. What is most important in assessing the United Nations is a balanced view of it. In the postwar period the expectations of the Japanese people in the United Nations was great. The whole legal structure concerning Japanese external policy, which was formed during the American occupation and at the time of the concluding of the Peace Treaty, was based on the ideal that Japanese security should be entrusted to the good will of international society or a supranational organization such as the United Nations. The U.S.-Japan Security Treaty, which is now essential to U.S.-Japan relations, was and still is supposed to be a temporary measure until such time as Japan's security could be placed in the hand of the United Nations. It was natural for the Japanese people to feel that their road to international isolation and the war started on the day the Japanese walked out of the League of Nations, that they were allowed to rejoin international society by being admitted to the United Nations, that they should respect the UN, and that they would never make the same mistake again. Also, international opinion and expectations for the UN were much higher than now, and perhaps highest at the time when Japan was admitted to the UN in 1956. Newly emerged Asian-African nations also joined the UN with high hopes and, recognizing this trend, big powers were interested in the political potentialities of the United Nations.

In Japan in that period, there was a strong trend of abstract and absolute pacifism, and there was, in one part of the population, an excessive expectation of the United Nations, since they wanted to realize the ideal of maintaining peace and security of Japan and the world without building a defense capability for Japan.

Overestimation begets underestimation. Now there is a tendency totally to neglect the UN, simply because we *cannot* trust the security of Japan to the UN. I feel that the underestimation is equally dangerous. The Soviet Union may know it best. Maybe it does not forget the lesson that United Nations forces were established during the Russian boycott of the UN. The Soviet Union stayed in the UN in spite of repeated condemnations of it by resolutions at the time of the Hungarian invasion and on other occasions and in spite of having to exercise its veto repeatedly. We must not underestimate the potential authority of an organ which is capable of reflecting the majority opinion of international society nor the danger of antagonizing a group of nations with that authority behind them.

If we keep the following points always in sight, we arrive at a right assessment of the United Nations: no illusion regarding the capability of the United Nations. For the time being we should exclude the possibility of any supranational function of the United Nations. True idealism for eternal peace should start from an accurate assessment of the limitations of the present UN and should seek a practical solution for the future. Nor should we ignore the United Nations. There always exists an undercurrent of idealism in international society, a hope for some supranational organization or world federation and a respect for international democracy. This undercurrent surfaces from time to time, and, at the existing stage of international society, it is likely to end up in an organization similar to the present UN. The most practical way is to strengthen the already existing organization. The strengthening of UN functions constitutes a question to which every member state must have tried at least once to find an answer. The accumulation of experience is enormous. Also, in spite of repeated frustrations, some full or partial successes have been experienced. In any case, we can safely expect the United Nations Organization will survive for many years to come, always with the potential of playing some role in international politics.

But peace cannot be gained merely by desiring it. It requires effort and compensation. The power of the United Nations is the sum total of the power each member state is willing to contribute to it. If Japan wishes to have UN protection for its security, we cannot rule out other countries seeking the same protection from the UN. In that circumstance, Japan will not be permitted to ask military protection of the UN, which is based on the sum of military contributions of other countries, while at the same time Japan refuses to contribute its military power for the protection of other countries. Of course, under its constitution Japan has a policy of not engaging in military activities outside its borders, but this does not exempt Japan from its responsibilities. In order to make equitable contribution to the peace of the world, Japan must make the maximum contribution within the scope permissible under its constitution.

Disarmament. Disarmament has been discussed always in connection with detente, convergence, or even the North-South problem. Here let us concentrate on the practical problem only. First of all, the main issues of disarmament at present are nuclear disarmament or nuclear arms control, a matter to be dealt with primarily by nuclear powers, specifically by the United States and the USSR. Although Japan's role in the disarmament question is thus very limited and subsidiary, Japan may still be able to contribute to it in the following manner.

First, we could lay stress on the disastrous effects of nuclear weapons and on the necessity to avoid nuclear war from a moral, not political point of view. Of course, knowledge of the disastrous effects of the nuclear weapon is not a monopoly of the Japanese people. The nuclear powers, which have tested far more powerful bombs than the Hiroshima-Nagasaki type, should know better than Japan about it. Nor are all Japanese opposed to nuclear weapons. Some people are criticized as having abandoned Japan's opposition to nuclear weapons in general because they took an ideological stand in defense of Chinese nuclear tests while attacking American nuclear armaments. Also, being far short of significant political power, there exists a minority which supports Japanese nuclear armament. As a whole, however, Japan may still be called a unique country in the sense that it has adopted a policy of nonnuclear armament, and it is not expected to change its policy in the foreseeable future, in spite of the fact it has no legal limitation against nuclear armament as in the case of West Germany, and despite its economic strength. This special condition of Japan might give Japan the moral right to call for nuclear disarmament.

Secondly, Japan should behave with responsibility as the second largest economic power in the free world. Recognizing the fact that the present peace of the world depends upon the nuclear balance, we should take a practical attitude of supporting the balanced disarmament of not only nuclear weapons but also of other armaments. A small power may support an impractical proposal, on the grounds that it is only a domestic gesture or other reason, but Japan should always take into consideration the security of the whole world and engage in practical thinking. At the same time Japan should fully support the reasonable position of the free world.

Thirdly, as the country has no intention of becoming a nuclear power, Japan should defend the interests of nonnuclear powers. We should be watchful that the U.S.-USSR accords do not exceed the purpose of the maintenance of world peace and that they do not create an artificial inequality between nuclear and nonnuclear powers.

Fourthly, in shaping Japanese foreign policy, we should not overestimate the prospect for disarmament any more than the future of the United Nations. If we expect some progress to be gained by Japanese participation in a disarmament conference, it is a gross overestimation which carries with it the danger of frustration and future underestimation of efforts at disarmament. We expect many problems to be solved before the success of the presently negotiated arms control but, even if that control does achieve complete success, it is no more than the maintenance of the status quo, together with collateral measures, and it has a long, long way to go to real reduction of armaments and finally to total and complete disarmament. It would be already an overoptimistic prediction if we expect total and complete disarmament to be achieved in the next generation. Meanwhile it is necessary and inevitable that we have to rely on the deterrent capability for peace and security. The argument that "It is a contradiction to profess to support disarmament and at the same time to strengthen the self-defense force" is infantile. If one examines what kind of arms control will be feasible in the coming ten years, what effects such measures will have on Japanese security and the objective defense necessity of Japan in that period, this kind of argument is unthinkable. Moreover, in proceeding toward a complete and total disarmament, the strengthening of the peace-keeping function of the United Nations should be promoted at the same time. In that eventuality Japan may have to make a concrete contribution to cooperate with the peace-keeping function of the UN, not simply appealing to the peace of the world as in disarmament negotiations. Mental preparation for that eventuality may already be in order.

5

Japan and the Communist World

Detente and Deterrence

As we have seen we can summarize the development of detente in Europe as follows: First, peaceful coexistence was established as an agreement to avoid a total nuclear war between the United States and the Soviet Union; thus a possibility of war was almost eliminated on the European front, which is the most likely place to touch off a nuclear war in case of a serious conflict. All the leaders on both sides of the iron curtain came to believe there is no other way than either maintaining the status quo or seeking a peaceful settlement. All the people in Europe were freed from the fear of another war and various exchanges have been promoted in this relaxed atmosphere. There was certainly a change of mood after the Czechoslovakian invasion. The hope and expectation for a better world was high before that invasion, and immediately after there was news of the deep frustration from which East European intellectuals suffered. From the point of view of international politics, however, detente in the middle of the 60s is the same as that at the beginning of the 70s, since both of them are based on the status quo and the peaceful settlement of problems.

The question is whether it is possible to realize the same kind of detente in Asia or in the region around Japan. From the above summary we could draw a still briefer conclusion that detente can be achieved by starting with minimizing the danger of a war. This is, however, not the answer to the question. The real question is: What is the best way to minimize the danger of war—strengthening the UN, a good neighbor diplomacy, or deterrent capability? The obvious answer is to employ all methods concurrently. I do not agree with an abstract or ideological argument (ideological distinction between pacifism and militarism, a belief in force or conscience, and so on) such as "the maintenance of a deterrent capability contradicts a policy of good neighborly relations," or "a good neighborly policy could be an alternative to the deterrent capability." All the countries are maintaining a certain kind of deterrent capability. If these two concepts contradict each other, there will be no good neighborly diplomacy.

In concurrently applying all the methods for minimizing the danger of a war, their respective priority differs according to the state with which we are dealing. What we must recognize here is that a factor of force is very important in dealing with a Communist state. The reason is very simple; Communists put primary emphasis on force.

In deciding their fundamental policy and tactics—usually it takes the form of a Party program—Communists first make an objective analysis of the current situation. This is a kind of counterpart to our own efforts of analysis and predictions about our world. The central theme of this assessment is invariably the power relationship between revolutionary and antirevolutionary forces, i.e., between Communist and capitalist forces.

The Chinese Communists use violent expressions, such as, "The seizure of power by armed force, the settlement of the issue by war, is the central task and the highest form of revolution." This Marxist-Leninist principle of revolution holds good universally for China and for all other countries—"Mao's red book"—but in practice they are extremely careful about the assessment of power relations. The same book says, "Fight no battle unprepared, fight no battle you are not sure of winning; make every effort to be well prepared for each battle, make every effort to ensure victory in the given set of conditions as between the enemy and ourselves." In their guerrilla warfare the Chinese Red Army did not hesitate at all to retreat when they were not convinced of a sure victory.

In a sense Communists are reliable people. The most dangerous person you could fight is a mad person. You are at a disadvantage if you fight a person who is not afraid of going to prison or of dying. Communists are practical and rational people in this sense. They would not start a war without calculation for a sure victory and with a determination "to jump out from the high Balcony of Kiyomizu temple," a Zen aphorism for detachment from the yoke of worldly preoccupation, attributed to General Tojo who is said to have quoted it in determining to attack Pearl Harbor. Communists are always careful not to commit the error of infantilistic adventurism. Incidentally, during the Tet offensive in 1968, one of my colleagues, an expert on communism and sympathetic to the Vietcong, exclaimed that it was an infantile adventure which would destroy all the Communist organizations and structures in the South, which had been hitherto carefully hidden. The Tet offensive made a tremendous impact on the course of the Vietnam War, which no Communist experts had expected—an impact through American public opinion—but it appears now that the Vietcong "paid the price" in a way this observer had predicted.

When the power situation is clear, Communists have the ability to opt for peace, easily disregarding questions of "face" or past commitments. They also have the ability to use force without regard to any international agreement to which they are committed, world opinion, or universal morals.

Khrushchev took away the missiles from Cuba in spite of the possibility of a serious loss of face. In fact his action was severely criticized by the Chinese for both the adventurism and eventual retreat. Stalin gave up his assistance to Greek Communist guerrillas, reportedly in order to avoid a confrontation with the United States and Great Britain on the question of influence in Greece, which Stalin judged essential for control of the Mediterranean sea.

On the other hand, Brezhnev invaded Czechoslovakia. An overwhelming majority of observers and commentators in international affairs predicted no invasion for many convincing reasons, such as the reaction of world opinion, the possibility of further weakening of the international Communist movement, being contrary to the trend of peaceful coexistence and detente, and so on. A very few did predict the invasion. The Soviets' reasons for the invasion? (1) Czechoslovakia would not resist, (2) the United States would not come to help, and (3) the Soviet Union was very well aware of facts (1) and (2). Even so, the Soviet Union executed it with a tremendous number of troops and with a perfect rapidity.

In sum, the element of force, i.e., deterrent capability, has a fundamental importance in minimizing the possibility of a war with a Communist country. We return once more to the simple truth that peaceful coexistence is no more than another aspect of nuclear deterrence. The objective here is to point out that Japan should not neglect the importance of deterrent capability in its efforts to achieve a stable peace in Asia. Of course in the case of Japan, it is not foreseeable that Japan would arm itself with nuclear deterrent capabilities. The deterrent capability of Japan is to be found in its limited armed strength and in cooperative relations with the United States. Departure from this basic structure of the Japanese security policy might endanger the very base of detente itself.

Possibility of Detente in Asia

Japan seeks detente and a stable peace in Asia. Maintaining stability and peace in Asia constitutes a problem which international society has so far failed to achieve in the quarter century since the end of the world war. It is the worst area in East-West relations, where large-scale East-West wars were fought twice, and even now two governments are competing for legitimacy in many divided nations and the tension between them still remains high. I do not think its solution is easy, but there may be opportunities for achieving detente as international conditions change. It is not my aim here to suggest a policy alternative for Japan for promoting detente in Asia. A policy should be based on the correct assessment of the situation existing at the time of its application. Suggesting a policy would serve little purpose as long as we are not certain about the future situation. Here we are examining the factors which should not be ignored when we discuss the possibility of detente in Asia in the foreseeable future. After the events of the early 70s, such as Sino-American and Sino-Japanese normalization and the Vietnam cease-fire, I contemplated whether I ought to modify my original observations about the situation of Asia, I have decided not to do so. These events certainly opened the gate to detente, but nobody is yet certain what will follow after the first steps. Anyway, the situation is still far different from the state achieved in Europe and I think I am still allowed to predict that the road to detente is not an easy one in Asia.

Relations with the Soviet Union

Concerning the Soviet Union, we may be able to say the same thing in Asia as we have said in Europe. Japan is playing a role as part of the overall American deterrent capability within the framework of the U.S.-Soviet peaceful coexistence. It is assumed that a full-scale military intervention by the Soviet Union on Japan would touch off a nuclear war with the same high probability as in Europe, because of Japan's own defense capability and the U.S.-Japan Security Treaty. Therefore we may say that the relation of peaceful coexistence in a narrow sense already exists between Japan and the Soviet Union. The problem of the Northern territories is certainly preventing the achievement of a stable friendly relation between Japan and the Soviet Union, but very few people believe in a war with the Soviet Union and various exchanges are being promoted. We may consider it a satisfactory situation in the context of East-West relations. The only thing we must remember is that we should not entertain the illusion that "deterrent capability is unnecessary because of prevailing peace," forgetting that the prevailing peace was achieved by that capability.

Peaceful Coexistence and Detente
in Asia

We have found it difficult to distinguish detente from peaceful coexistence. It is still more difficult to do so in Asia.

The expression "fluid" is often used to describe the situation in Asia. Nonuse of force and peaceful settlement of problems based on the status quo, which characterize the European state, can hardly be applied to the situation in Asia, particularly in Indo-China. In Vietnam, as well as in Cambodia and Laos, it is difficult even to define what the status quo is. If we really need a European-style solution based on the status quo, we must first visualize a certain state of affairs which has to be achieved as a policy objective based on realistic assessment of the situation and then, after achieving this, we have to find a way to maintain the status quo thus achieved. In other places, such as the 38th parallel and the Taiwan Strait, where the status quo is at the moment quite stable, the positions are far from formal recognition of the status quo, by both parties involved. Therefore, the possibility of the use of force still remains.

The reason why the situation in Asia is fluid lies in the difference itself between Europe and Asia. Asia is a much bigger region than Europe and, in the continental part of Southeast and South Asia, geographical conditions and existing transportation and military facilities set serious limitations on any modern mobile operations on a large scale; many countries are also protected by the sea. Before NATO was organized in 1949, the people in Bonn or in Paris or in Rome lived in a constant nightmare that their capitals might be overrun by the mobile divisions of the Red Army within a few days after the outbreak of war. In Asia, such fear has never been shared in common among the nations in the region, even in the early 50s or late 60s, when the shadow of China was quite strongly felt over these countries. This fact, and the heterogeneity in race, culture, historical background, and political institutions, limit the possibility of regional defense arrangements of the NATO type. Instead Asia has a different security problem, which requires somewhat different approaches from those that succeeded in Europe. In many countries, economies are still underdeveloped and fragile. Low standards of living and certain social situations, such as land ownership, expose the weakest flank of these countries to subversive activities.

In Europe, the situation is now so stabilized that any military action across the iron curtain is prevented by the possibility of incurring full-scale war and eventually nuclear war. On the other hand, Asia is still such a fluid region that two large-scale wars have been fought, one in Korea and one in Vietnam, without entailing a nuclear war and without the direct confrontation of two superpowers.

Now we know peaceful coexistence and detente in Europe are a product not only of the U.S.-Soviet nuclear balance, but also of the historical political, social, and economic background of European established industrial democracies which rule out the possibility of internal insurgence and guerrilla warfare and to which the only effective military threat is a full-scale military attack from outside; effective and rigid Soviet control of East Europe which also rules out the possibility of a voluntary change of system from inside; racial and cultural similarities of nations (the Soviet led solidarity of nations is added to this), geographical conditions and advanced transportation facilities which produce a condition of interdependence among the nations of both blocs. In short the combination of domestic stability in each nation and a high degree of interdependence among the nations of each bloc has created the necessary condition. This status quo can only be destroyed by a full-scale war.

How can we achieve a stable peace in the Asian regions around China? The ideal condition may be such that Asian nations achieve social and economic stability and maintain a system which can solve various domestic problems in more or less democratic procedures, and possess sufficient military capability to control guerrilla wars instigated from outside. If they succeed in gaining deterrent capability by regional alliances or by security arrangements with outside powers against a military threat greater than that presented by guerrilla action, their stability will be so much increased. And if finally they establish an internal and external condition which cannot be altered except by a full-scale exercise of force from outside, then they can expect a higher credibility of a nuclear umbrella from a superpower outside the region. Of course it is an ideal condition which many American policymakers dreamed of and tried to achieve and which they eventually ended up being frustrated by. In these days the impetuous attitude, trying to achieve something by massive American intervention and in a term of a few years, seems to have been abondoned. It is a fact, however, that the situation in Southeast Asia, except in Indochina, has been greatly improved in the past ten years, significantly owing to the repeated efforts of this kind. And the continued efforts to achieve more stabilization of these countries will remain of value for many years to come.

Therefore, what is required for Asian security are measures involving an entire spectrum of military, political, psychological, economic and social factors. They should be applied case by case and country by country, because each country differs from others in its stage of economic development and historical background, rather than an overall regional approach, as in the case of NATO countries. The usefulness of regional cooperation is limited and the bilateral relations with the United States or with Japan will continue to be important. Above all it takes time before a given measure will have any tangible result. Although Japan cannot contribute to the defense capabilities of these countries, it can contribute significantly to their stability in terms of their social, economic, and psychological development.

U.S.-China Peaceful Coexistence

My original observation in this chapter is obsolete. In the Japanese edition I wrote that there is little possibility of a relation of peaceful coexistence, such as the one achieved between the United States and the Soviet Union, being achieved between China and the USA, and, if any, there may be some kind of entente based on national interests of the two states. Then I explained at length the reason why Sino-American peaceful coexistence is difficult, based on the analysis of the stage of the Chinese nuclear development and geopolitical conditions surrounding China, making it unlikely to touch off a nuclear war as in Europe. These analyses may become useful again if either China goes back to its policy prior to 1971 or Sino-Soviet relations are mended, but at this moment I do not feel it necessary to burden the readers with this analysis. There seems to exist a certain kind of entente based on traditional power politics between the United States and China at present, but it may be too early to comment on it.

Sino-Japanese Relations

The Question of China and Taiwan

This book does not deal with the legal question of the rival governments for legitimacy. Particularly the question concerning China and Taiwan has long been an extremely sensitive question in Japan. We have always had strong public opinion favoring diplomatic normalization of Sino-Japanese relations and at the same time strong public opinion favoring the maintenance of relations with Taiwan. The Japanese government finally opted for diplomatic relations with China while preserving some practical relations with Taiwan, whereas the United States proceeded toward normalization of its relations with China while preserving diplomatic relations with Taiwan. It continues as a sensitive question in international politics and it is doubtful if such a question is worth discussing in this book, which is concerned primarily with the macropolitical trends in the world situation. As in the preceding cases of diplomatic recognition of China by France and other countries, the simple act of recognition does not much change the substance of state relations and still less affects the fundamental question, which is, what should be the relations between China and Japan as two states of different systems and what should be the relations between the Chinese nation and the Japanese nation in many decades to come.

The Question of Security

There is little problem of security of Japan vis-à-vis China, as long as we maintain our own defense capability and the U.S.-Japan Security Treaty. Although we might face a new situation when China is armed with effective ICBMs, it is hard to discuss its eventual importance because it still takes time for China to have enough capability to affect American nuclear strategy even partially and other future circumstances are still unknown to us. At present, in any case, the strategic circumstances in and out of China are not such that they allow China to take military action against Japan after "making every effort to be prepared for each battle and making every effort to ensure victory in the given set of conditions as between the enemy and the Chinese themselves."

A people's liberation war is not an effective threat either at present. We cannot possibly imagine a number of Japanese workers and farmers, who are presently enjoying the Japanese standard of living, taking up arms and leading guerrilla life in the mountains. Except for the schizophrenic case of the "United Red Army" of Japan, there is practically no security threat of guerrilla warfare in present day Japan, although in security questions we must not dismiss potential danger as the Japanese social situation changes in the future.

Special problems related to the broader question of security between Japan and China are: (1) the emotional element of the China question in Japan, and (2) the instability of Asian regions around China, their expectations from Japan and our responsibility.

Japan has a special problem with China in that public opinion favorable to China tends to be created quite easily. In Japan there exists nostalgia for the China mainland, friendly feeling toward Chinese who "write the same letters and belong to the same race," and the complex emotion that Japan was the "assailing party" in the Second World War. It is undeniable that some Japanese are liable to accept Chinese propaganda while rejecting the Soviet brand, even when they have the same substance. The fact that, in the Sino-Japanese communique of the "Memorandum Trade" signed before diplomatic normalization, they succeeded in putting in a sentence saying "the Japanese side considered it important that the U.S.-Japan Security Treaty is a threat to China, threat to the people of every nation in Asia and a great obstacle to the Sino-Japanese relation" proves this advantageous position of China. We cannot ignore the possibility that in the future China could create a division of opinion within Japan and thus an element of unstability in our domestic politics. The Japanese side could cope with it by improving the Japanese people's knowledge of China; that China is a nation of Chinese but at the same time it is a nation of Communists; that we should well recognize the fact that there exist elements of Communist tactics in the words and actions of China which we must carefully discern; that real friendship will be created not by accommodating to propaganda but by frankly presenting and recognizing the positions of each side.

There is some possibility of conflicts between Japan and Communist countries, such as China and the Soviet Union, concerning the Japanese role in the stability of Southeast Asia. It is an established policy of Japan, which does not make military contributions, to cooperate with Asian nations in their stability and prosperity by political and economic means. Until quite recently both China and Russia have criticized Japan for this kind of activity. If Communist forces aspire to revolution in these countries, it is natural that they do not welcome these countries continuing to enjoy their stability and prosperity, maintaining their existing systems, and that they criticize Japanese economic cooperation as economic imperialism. Against these charges Japan should stand firm. We should maintain the unfaltering belief that the stability of nation-states in Asia will contribute to minimizing the possibility of wars and disturbances in that region and will eventually form the basis of peace and stability of all Asia, including the China mainland. Japan should do its best to help achieve this objective. This attitude also applies to Japanese relations with Korea. It may happen that, as the Korean economy prospers and is being stabilized as the result of the effort of self-help of Korea itself, Japanese economic cooperation, and American security assurance, North Korea may feel uneasy and this uneasiness might sometimes lead to the heightening of tensions in the peninsula. However, if we succeed in maintaining the security and peace there by the effect of the sufficient deterrent capability, until South Korea attains genuine economic and social stability, then we can have a new prospect for lasting peace in the peninsula.

Conditions for Sino-Japanese
Peaceful Coexistence

As I pointed out in the chapter on peaceful coexistence, I see a chance for Sino-Japanese normalization at the time when China returns to the attitude of the mid-50s. The spirit of the mid-50s is represented in the five principles of peace declared by Chou En-lai and Nehru in 1954. This document is a practical and reasonable one, based on recognition of existing world conditions where two different systems coexist. Although these principles have been given low priority in the official attitude of China for a long period—the full decade of the 60s—I thought that it would be a practical approach to base the conditions of Sino-Japan relations on this document, which at least once constituted the center of the official Chinese position.

Among the five principles I particularly thought it essential to recognize mutually the difference in the systems of Japan and China. The differences in the two nations directly reflect the history of modernization of the two countries. Japan dashed ahead on the road of capitalism, experienced trial-and-error in its parliamentary democracy, and now belongs to the group of free industrial democracies. China became a Communist state through agrarian revolution and armed struggle. These are irrevocable historical facts. Japan wants a friendly relation with China, which understands well that there is almost zero probability for either a Communist revolution or Facist takeover in present day Japan. That means we want a friendship without false expectations or fear. The Sino-Japanese relation should be based on China and Japan as they are. Furthermore, I thought that the principle of nonintervention, particularly in connection with Chinese propaganda toward Japan, was important for a better Sino-Japanese relationship. Chinese propaganda was sometimes vehement. It often called upon the Japanese people to rise against the Japanese government and urged Japanese traders in Peking to criticize the current policy of their own government. Japan, while not believing the Chinese system any better than ours, has not called upon the Chinese people to rise against their own government. I believed that, in that context, the propriety was ours and called upon China to refrain from making unnecessary propaganda.

These conditions may be already obsolete. In fact it appears that China did return on many points to the position it held in the mid-50s, at least as far as its attitude toward Japan is concerned. China appears to have accommodated to Japan as it is, moreover, even by acquiescing in the maintenance of the U.S.-Japan Security Treaty and, by stopping its criticism and propaganda against Japan. The only thing I can hope now is that the present Sino-Japanese relation will be maintained in the future, surviving many international events, as a basis to govern the Sino-Japanese relations in the coming years.

Some Thoughts on the Sino-Japanese
Convergence

The possibility of Sino-Japanese detente based on the economic theory of convergence is obviously very remote. The scenario of evolution to an optimum economic society and political, ideological convergence is not applicable to the relations between Chinese society and Western society, like the United States and Japan. Even if possible, it would take generations. This is also a North-South question. As we have seen, it is dangerous to connect directly the rise in the living standard of a nation with its more peaceful tendency. We could assume that a nation whose per capita income is 2,000 dollars needs a status quo and peace because each of its citizens has too much to lose. But we cannot tell which will be felt as a greater threat by the neighboring nations, a China of per capita income of 100 dollars or one of 200 dollars. North Korea in the late 60s, when the U.S.-North Korean relations were quite tense through various incidents, was calculated to have had a per capita income of 200 dollars. Discounting the difference of age and system, it may be clear in the examples of Japan at the Meiji Restoration and the one right before the Second World War that higher per capita income does not necessarily mean a lesser threat to neighboring countries. The logical conclusion from the above analysis is that we must wait for the time when China achieves a sufficiently high per capita income, and meanwhile we have to maintain a sufficient deterrent capability. The time required for it, however, is impractically long.

On the other hand an approach which puts emphasis on the historical and cultural tradition is more easily applicable to Sino-Japan relations and in fact many people do take this approach. As General De Gaulle called France and Russia sisters of European civilization, Japan and China share the same source of civilization, use the same characters, and belong to the same Mongoloid race, perhaps for a long time after the ideology lapses. Some people point out the difference in modernization in the past few hundred years and the superficiality of the resemblance. It is also a fact that the cultural revolution tended to deny the traditional values of China. It would serve no purpose to discuss the true character of Chinese and Japanese civilizations here. Mutual understanding of nations is valuable between any two countries and we should exhaust all possibilities for that. It is certainly possible to improve mutual understanding between individuals by quoting Chinese classics, which are the common heritage of both nations. Traditional oriental morals or virtue would also help develop mutual understanding. One caveat is in order, however. If we rely on these traditional elements exclusively and overestimate them, we are bound to hit an insurmountable obstacle of ideology. Many people who tried to bridge a better Sino-Japanese relation in the past have encountered ideological obstacles in the course of their endeavors. The detente policy of General De Gaulle, while based on the relations between nations and states, presupposes a lapse in ideology. As long as the ideological difference exists between Japan and China, the Sino-Japanese relation should be based on a balance of national interests of two nations, presupposing that the political and economic systems of the two nations are quite different.

Liberalization or a tendency to be moderate does not necessarily require a high living standard. Some Chinese literature, which appeared in the period before the cultural revolution, is comparable or even superior to Russian liberal literature in its criticism and subtle sarcasm on existing authority. Liberalization is essentially a political question. It is more influenced by political and social circumstance than by economic standard. Particularly, the openness of the society, or, conversely, the strictness of the control on freedom of speech has vital importance for it. When the Chinese people freely read books which contain thoughts other than Communist ideology, see societies other than their own, and are allowed to express their choice for a desirable society, we will have a different world. There would not be much difference between the choices of human beings. Of course there is a good possibility that the Chinese people would opt after all for a system somewhat similar to their own at present, considering the differences in the stage of economic development and various circumstances between Chinese society and ours. I think it would be fair enough. In that case they are not ideologically doctrinarian, insisting categorically that the Communist system should be applied to China and all other countries universally. Of course it is still a dream world. Political power can close the window on people as it likes. What we should do is to increase the various exchanges with China so that Chinese people can get as much information as possible about the outside world. Any exchange and intercourse would be useful. This is not a tactic or strategy in East-West relations, but an authentic approach for improving mutual understanding, which is basic for friendly relations between any states.

The World Detente and Japan

Conditions for an Ideal World

Japan is a country which needs peace in the world more than any nation because of its economic structure, which requires free trade and safe passage of goods and materials all over the world. The Japanese Constitution sets out in its preamble an ideal world in which Japan could entrust its own security to the justice and fairness of other nations. The only possible form of international society in which this ideal might be achieved should be based on complete and total disarmament and on the effective peace-keeping capability of the United Nations. In fact Khrushchev once suggested this. Although it was virtually withdrawn subsequently, we could still learn some lessons from the course of debate on this proposal and related issues. We could tell under what international circumstance these would be achieved; that is, in the case where all the countries with significant power, including of course the United States and the USSR, share the same values—the same vision concerning the most desirable form of the world—and are willing to cooperate with each other, or, are made to cooperate out of necessity for survival.

In this context of supranational cooperation the necessity for sharing a common value is obvious. For example, under total and complete disarmament, both the United States and the Soviet Union are supposed to transfer control over a substantial portion of their armed forces to the United Nations at some stage of its progress. The policy of the United Nations is, after all, the policy of the people who control the United Nations. If the values of these people were based on Communist ideology and their ultimate aim was world revolution, the United States would certainly refuse to surrender its armies to them. If vice-versa, the Soviet Union would not. The Soviet Union once proposed a so-called troika formula, but since it is based on the existence of the two systems, it would not be able to agree to anything on which people have different values. In more practical questions, such as full inspection on disarmament, compulsory jurisdiction of the International Court of Justice, limitation on the veto in the Security Council, acceptance of them by the Soviet Union would be tantamount to the abandonment of its protective precautions against the capitalist world, and therefore should be very difficult to be realized.

As we have seen, the road to the convergence of two value systems is long. It is frustrating to see how the Soviet Union has reacted against Western detente policy since 1966 within and without its own country and how the Chinese have professed to maintain their revolutionary spirit in the cultural revolution. However, if we seek an ideal form of international society, we have no alternative other than to expect ideology to lapse sometime in future. It will take a long time. But I believe it worth while for any policy planner to think over a possible form of an ideal world from time to time, while being careful not to confuse it with an immediate national interest and above all not to give it a priority over fundamental national interests.

Domestic Politics

Finally all problems come back to Japan itself. The detente policy of the Western world was possible only when it was based on the confidence that the free democratic system was superior to the existing Communist system. The Western side could continue its policy of detente because of its confidence that the people of Western nations would not opt for a Communist system while the people in Communist nations might be attracted by the Western system when the peoples of both sides are completely exposed to each other and given free choice of a system they like. The West is also confident that Eastern society may face serious impacts from the introduction of the freedom of expression which the Western societies can easily survive. What is necessary for Japan is this confidence. We have to be always confident that the Japanese people would prefer living in Japan to living under the dictatorial systems such as China and Russia. If Japan were to close the window and try to limit the knowledge of Japanese people concerning the Communist world to the forced labor camps, only then could we say that Japan had lost the peaceful competition.

What is necessary for achieving and maintaining this confidence? It is, of course necessary to maintain economic stability and prosperity. The proud, peaceful coexistence policy of Khrushchev was based on the fact or at least on the hope that the Eastern economic growth rate was superior to the West in the 1950s and that they might catch up with the United States economically sometime in the future. The economies of Russia and China failed as early as the beginning of the 60s, and instead it was the Western nations, above all Japan, which enjoyed the golden 60s. It was at that time that detente policy was initiated by the Western side.

The ups and downs in economy, however, are inevitable. All international events have worked in favor of Japan in the past years, but there is no guarantee that it will be like this in the future. Even the most optimistic economist should modify his forecast if the Western nations, above all the United States, turn to protectionism. Some unfavorable results of rapid growth, such as pollution and inflation, might also affect the fundamental structure of existing economic systems.

Will the Japanese people keep confidence in the present system in case of such economic havoc? Although it depends on the extent of the damage, I am quite confident about the future. In the Great Depression, the United States did not turn Communist or Facist, but endeavored to rehabilitate its economy by the New Deal within the traditional political framework, while Japan moved toward expansionism for the solution. What would happen in Japan in a similar case? Japan's situation today is remarkably different from that of the 30s. We now have a much stronger economic structure and a much better established democracy in all parts of the Japanese society than in the 30s. I would imagine that Japan would try to overcome economic difficulty within the framework of the present free political system, and to avoid any drift toward a dictatorial system, either rightist or leftist.

It is perhaps presumptuous to predict the future of Japan but, at least as a policy, we must try to preserve the present free democratic system in Japan. The conclusion I have drawn at the end of the chapter on detente policy should also apply to the case of Japan. So far as international relations are concerned there is nothing certain yet to which we can trust Japanese security—nothing in the future perspectives of Communist countries and nothing in the possibility of an effective supranational organization. We definitely cannot count on a simple linear progression toward peace and reason. Things might take a turn for the worse with almost the same probability as for the better. Very likely we will find ourselves in a world which is not so different from ours after several decades and even in the next century. Nothing is certain enough for Japan to abandon its security arrangements for deterrent purposes. On the other hand, we are at least responsible for what will happen in Japan itself. In this era of nuclear stalemate, where peace is preserved by the system of mutual deterrence, the development of the domestic side of politics in each country is as important as its foreign policy in the context of peace and war. An abrupt decay of a system has always been a major cause of international tension as seen in many instances in this century. We can, and should, see that the social and political evolution of Japan will not become a factor detrimental to the peace and security of the world. It requires a constant effort to maintain and improve the democratic system based on freedom of speech, freedom of assembly, respect for human rights, and to make our society more effective, more stable, and more in harmony with the global environment. We should not be afraid of progress. The Western side was on the offensive in the convergence theory because, while the Eastern side dogmatically denied the possibility of the evolution of the Eastern system, the Western side took a flexible attitude that it could accommodate the evolution of its own system if that meant peaceful change under democratic rule and if it meant progress for the society. We must maintain an effective deterrent capability and keep our democratic society both stable and flexible, closely guarding the peace and prosperity of Japan. As the future unfolds, we still have to expect many vicissitudes, until the time when the world will finally achieve a lasting structure of peace.

Index

Index

Adventurism, 19
Afro-Asian Conference, in Bandung, 33
Amalrik, A., 73
Anarchism, theory of, 73
Anti-Vietnam campaigns, 29
Antiwar campaigns, 28, 29
Appeasement policy, Chamberlain's, 2
Arab-Israeli conflict, 30
Asia, detente in, 97-100
  economic stability of, 99-101
  European influence in, 83
  Japanese role in, 102
  Peaceful coexistence in, 98-100
  people's liberation movements in, 31
Atomic bombs, 16. *See also* Nuclear weapons

Bakunin, Michael, 73
Balance of interests, 88-91
Bandung diplomacy, 12, 33-38
Bangladesh, Russian support for, 32
Bauer, B., 13
Berlin Wall crisis, 3, 50
Bernstein, E., 13
Bolsheviki, 24
Bourgeoisie, ideology of, 65, 67
  support of, 31, 32
Brandt Administration, 53, 75
Bratislava Conference, 79, 82
Bregel, E., 62, 63-65, 66, 71
Brezhnev, Leonid, 12
  and Czechoslovakian invasion, 21, 96
  at 23rd Party Congress, 29-30
Brezhnev doctrine, 4, 20, 48
Brezhnev regime, literary activity in, 71
  peaceful transition in, 25
Brzezinski, Zbigniew, 66

Cambodia, status quo in, 89
Capitalism, 60
  creeping, 69
  salvation of, 65
Caribbean, 1
Chamberlain, Neville, 2
Cherbakov, V., 63
China, cultural revolution in, 39, 40,
  66, 68-69, 75, 77, 81, 85, 106
  domestic conditions of, 85-86
  domestic policies of, 39, 40
  economic growth of, 75, 86
  economy of, 39
  flexibility of, 35, 37, 38, 40
  Japanese attitudes toward, 101
  as nuclear power, 86
  and peaceful coexistence, 55, 85
  peace diplomacy of, 12
  prestige of, 14
  revolutionary diplomacy of, 32
  and Taiwan, 100-101
  Tito-ization of, 83
Chinese Communists, 17, 96
Chinese diplomacy, flexibility of, 39
Chou En-lai, at Bandung Conference, 33-34
  peace principles of, 103
  on Sino-Japanese relations, 35
  at 10th National Congress, 5
Cisař, Čestmir, 26
Class struggle, 19. *See also* People's liberation movements
Cold War, and industrial system, 61
Collectivization, 85
Colonial liberation movement, 19
Communism, changes in, 60, 72, 77
  international, 25, 28
  and mass consumption, 59
  as "outdated ideology," 57
  theoretical, 11, 12-14
Communist, The, 29
Communist party, Chinese, 19, 31
  Japanese, 27
  Pakistan, 32
  Western, 8
Communists, Chinese, 17, 96
  force and, 95
Communist society, future of, 77
  metamorphosis in, 69
Communist states, domestic
  conditions of, 84-86
  ideological struggles in, 67
  and Japan, 89, 95-108
Competition, economic, 90
Confrontation, military, 1
  recognition of, 65
Confucius, 2

111

113

Europe, common heritage of, 48
  division of, 55
  peaceful coexistence in, 47
  stabilization of, 99
  Western front in, 21
European framework, 48, 66, 104

Five-Antis, 39
Five principles, 33-34, 35, 39, 103
Flexibility, of diplomacy, 5
Force, Khrushchevian view of, 24
Foreign policy, definition of, 83
  Japanese, 79-80
  realistic analysis of, 81, 82
Freedom, intellectual, 71, 72, 74, 105
Fundamentals of Scientific
  Communism, 20

Galbraith, J.K., 60, 61, 63, 64, 70
Game theory, 21-22
Geneva Conference, of 1954, 39
German-Rumanian normalization, 52
Germany, threat of, 56
  unification of, 47, 48, 49, 50, 51, 55
  after Versailles Treaty, 89
Great Depression, 107
Great Leap, 86
  failure of, 39
Greece, Soviet influence in, 96
GNP, Japanese, 80

Hallstein doctrine, 52
Hatoyama cabinet, 39
Hawks, 8
Hundred Flowers, 39
Hungary, invasion of, 21, 24, 26, 70,
  92

ICBMs, Chinese, 101
  Soviet development of, 58
Ideology, 19
  decline of, 77
  effect of, 89
  and technology, 64
Ikeda, Prime Minister, 80
Ikeda Cabinet, low posture policy of,
  40
India, China's relations with, 34-35
Indo-China, status quo in, 98
Industrialization, promotion of, 67
Industrial systems, 60, 61, 64, 70

Industry, concentration on, 84
Inflation, 107
Intermediary zone, 36
International Court of Justice, 106
Iron triangle, 52
Ishibashi cabinet, 38,
  40
Isolationism, of Japan, 81
  of 1930s, 87

Japan, American occupation of, 91
  and Asian detente, 97-100
  and China, 35, 40-41, 101
  and Communist World, 89, 95-108
  defense necessity of, 94
  democratic system in, 107
  domestic politics of, 106-108
  as economic power, 89, 93
  economy of, 80, 107
  foreign policy of, 79-80
  GNP of, 80
  isolationism of, 91
  military activities of, 80, 93
  peace diplomacy of, 79-94
  and Sino-Soviet relations, 87-88
  and world detente, 105-108
Japanese Communist Party, 27
Japanese-Korean Treaty, 8, 40
Japanese-Taiwan Treaty, 35
JCP. See Japanese Communist Party
Johnson, President Lyndon B., 8
  bombing halt announcement of, 82
  bridge-building proposal by, 63
  and detente policy, 47-49, 50
Johnson Administration, 87

Kennedy, President John F., 2
  and Cuban crisis, 21
Kennedy Administration, 87
Khrushchev, Premier Nikita, assessment
  of, 14
  and Cuban missile crisis, 96
  and disarmament, 105
  and Hungarian invasion, 21
  liberalization of, 68, 70, 71
  peaceful coexistence of, 50
  20th CPSU Congress speech of,
    12-13, 14, 20, 22, 23, 24
  22nd CPSU Congress report of, 26,
    28
  Khrushchevian theory, 11, 14-29

objectives of, 52, 56
Oxford Union, 2

Pacifism, absolute, 81, 92
Pacifist philosophers, attitudes of, 21
Pakistan, and China, 32
Paper tigers, 19
Paris talks, on Vietnam, 5
Peace, as low tension, 76
  as Soviet policy, 29
  U.N. and, 92
Peace diplomacy, Japanese, 79-94
Peaceful coexistence, 2, 9, 77
  in Asia, 98-100
  Brezhnevian definition of, 44
  Chinese attitude on, 16, 19, 34, 36,
    55, 85
  definition of, 11
  vs. detente policy, 44-46
  establishment of, 95
  Khrushchevian, 12
  Marxist-Leninist approach to, 65
  necessity for, 64
  and people's liberation movements,
    29-30, 31
  Sino-American, 100
  Sino-Japanese, 102-103
  Soviet, 14, 15-22, 37, 74, 84
  as strategy, 18
Peaceful competition, 22-23, 77
  during Brezhnev period, 23
Peaceful transition, 23-26
Peace movement, and peaceful
  coexistence, 28
Peace Notes, 46
  importance of, 49-50
  Russian reply to, 51
Peace offensive, 6
People's Commune, 39
People's liberation movements, 15,
  20-32
  in China, 85
  definition of, 30
  invincibility of, 82
  in Japan, 101
  support for, 34
Poland, invasion of, 2
  and West Germany, 52
Polish-German Treaty (1972), 53
Political systems, and economic
  systems, 66
Pollution, 107

Power politics, 66, 76
  detente policy as, 45
  Sino-American, 100
Poznan incident, 70
Poznan riots, 26
Prague Spring, 4, 26, 70. *See also*
  Czechoslovakian invasion
Productivity, as economic measure, 59
Proletarian dictatorship, 27
Propaganda, 14, 77
  Chinese, 103
  Communist, 12
  by posture, 8

Quemoy, bombardment of, 39

Red Army, 6
Re-Stalinization, 20
Revanchism, German, 53
Revisionists, 13
Revolution, Maoist concept of, 25
  socialist, 24, 25
  spiritual, 69
  world, 12, 22
Revolutionary theory, equality and
  liberty in, 73
Rostow, W.W., 58, 59, 64
Russian revolution, 23
Russians, and Chinese, 33. *See also*
  Sino-Soviet relations
Russo-Japanese relations, 90, 98. *See
  also* Sino-Soviet relations

Sakharov, Andrei D., 73, 76
  convergence theory of, 66-68
SALT, 2, 21
Sato cabinet, 38, 40
Second strike capability, Soviet, 16
Security Council, veto in, 106
Siberia, 4
Sino-American relations, 36-38, 100
  importance of, 41
  normalization of, 97
  reversal in, 84
  and Taiwan, 101
Sino-Indian border, 14, 32
Sino-Indian Treaty, of 1954, 34
Sino-Japanese relations, 33, 37-38,
  100-105
  and Chinese flexibility, 35
  disruption of, 40
  in mid-1950s, 38

Sino-Japanese relations *(Cont.)*
  normalization of, 36, 97
  stability of, 41
Sino-Japanese war, 31
Sino-Soviet dispute, 14, 15, 25, 83
  language of, 18
Sino-Soviet polemics, 32-33
Sino-Soviet relations, 33, 41, 89-90
  and Japan, 87-88
  worsening of, 32
Social democracy, German, 63
Social Democrats, in Czechoslovakia, 72
Socialism, 11, 22
  alternative ways to, 13, 25, 26, 70
  building of, 85
  capitalistic evolution of, 65
  economic system of, 58
  productive system of, 20
Socialist revolution, 24, 25
Socioeconomic system, mixed, 63
  single, 66, 67. *See also* Convergence
    theory
Solzhenitzin, Alexander, 71
Southeast Asia, Japanese role in, 102
Soviet-French Declaration, 48
Soviet-German Treaty (1972), 53
Soviet Union, changes in, 72
  and Cuban crisis, 103
  decision-making in, 13
  and detente policy, 44, 46
  domestic conditions of, 84-85
  and Eastern bloc solidarity, 52
  economic growth of, 58-59, 85
  economic reform of, 58, 69, 70, 72, 84
  economy of, 59, 71
  foreign policy structure of, 14-29
  ideological education in, 77
  industrial production of, 23
  and Japan, 98
  liberalization of, 70
  literary traditions of, 73
  living standard in, 85
  nuclear capability of, 16
  peace offensive of, 6-7
  prestige of, 14
  strengthening of, 22-23
  and U.N., 92
Soviet-Yugoslavian rapprochement, 26
Sputnik, 23, 58

Stalin, Joseph, 17
  criticism of, 70, 71, 84
  and Greek Communists, 96
  Khrushchev and, 13
Standard of living, 104
  high, 91
  Japanese, 101
  low, 99
  Soviet, 85
State and Revolution, 73
States, Marxist-Leninist, 14
Status quo, maintenance of, 51, 53, 54, 85, 91, 95, 98
Stockholm Appeal, 6
Strategy, peaceful coexistence as, 18
Submergence theory, 59
Sun-tzu, 22
Svoboda, L., 72

Tactics, of peace offensive, 7
Taiwan, China and, 100-101
  Japanese relations with, 35, 36, 41
Taiwan Strait, 98
Tanaka, Prime Minister, 35, 36
Technology, and ideology, 64
Technostructure, 61
Tension, 1-5
  aggravation of, 7
  low, 76
Tet offensive, of North Vietnam, 82, 96
Thermonuclear warfare, 15
Three-Antis, 39
"Three peaces," 14-15
Tinbergen, J., 58, 60, 64
  and peaceful coexistence, 65
Togliatti, P., 17-18
Trade, Japan-Taiwan, 89
  Memorandum, 38, 39, 40, 102
  Sino-Japanese, 39, 40, 41, 88, 89
Trade balance, of U.S., 87
Trade relations, with China, 35
  improving, 30
Transition, 17
20th CPSU Congress, 12-13, 20, 24, 33
21st CPSU Congress, 23
"Two entireties," 14-15

United Nations, peace-keeping
  capability of, 105

policy of, 106
role of, 91-93
strengthening of, 94, 95
United Red Army, of Japan, 101
United States, Chinese
  rapprochement with, 86 (*see also*
  Sino-American relations)
  and detente policy, 46
  domestic conditions of, 86-87
  era of, 87
U.S. Japan Security Treaty, 7, 76, 91,
  98, 101
  as threat to Chinese, 102, 103
U.S.-North Korea relations, 104
U.S.-Soviet detente, 20. *See also*
  Detente

Versailles Treaty, 89
Vietnam, cease-fire in, 97
  peace settlement in, 81
  people's liberation movement of, 32
  status quo in, 98

Warsaw talks, with China, 5
Welfare economics, 60
West Germany, and detente, 49-51
  diplomacy of, 46
  and nuclear armament, 93
  Ostpolitik of, 51-53, 54
  Peace Notes of, 46, 49-50, 51
  revanchism of, 63
World, political environment of, 83-88
World Communist Party, peace appeal
  of, 28
World Congress for the Defense of
  Peace, 6
World government, 67
World Labor Federation, 28
World Peace Council, 6, 28

Yoshida cabinet, 38
Yugoslavia, political system of, 72
  rapprochement with, 25, 26

Zig-zag movement, 84, 86

About the Author

Hisahiko Okazaki, presently Counselor at the Japanese Embassy in Korea, received his training at Tokyo University and Cambridge University. He has served continuously in the Japanese Ministry of Foreign Affairs since 1955, his posts including Tokyo, London, Manila, Paris, Washington, and Seoul. An on-the-spot observer of international diplomacy, Mr. Okazaki has published articles on foreign affairs and a book in Japanese on the theory of detente.